Bread Blessed and Broken for the World

A Pastor's Reflections on the Celebration of Mass

Paulson Mundanmani

Table of Contents

Dedication

I dedicate this book to my parents in memoriam.

I am grateful to God for their endless support as I

journeyed towards my priesthood. They have

inspired me to be the person that I am.

Acknowledgments

This book represents the fruit of my many years of rewarding ministry as a priest. Throughout the writing and publishing process, many individuals from the community have taken time to help me bring it to completion. I give special thanks to the Christ the King Parish Community, Pleasant Hill, California. They have had a positive impact on my ministry as a person and a priest.

I am grateful to Bishop Michael Barber of the Diocese of Oakland, who allowed me to take a sabbatical, which made it possible for me to write this book, and for his feedback. I am especially grateful to the priests who are with me and who remain an inspiration—Fr. Brian Timoney, Fr. Vince Cotter, Fr. Mike Dibble, Fr. Tom Burns, Fr. Brian Joyce, and Fr. Mario Rizzo, who has brought us new energy as he begins his priesthood. They encouraged me to write this book, gifting me with their time to read the manuscript and offer their valuable input.

I also thank Alfred Garrotto for translating my dream into a finished book—editing and preparing the completed manuscript and seeing it through to publication. I am grateful to the staff of Christ the King community who are the most dedicated team I have worked with. A number of parishioners and friends have read my manuscript and offered their feedback. To them I say, thank you.

Foreword

After 25 years of ministry in the priesthood, Oakland Bishop Michael Barber gave me the gift of a sabbatical. I spent two months in Latin America learning Spanish in one of the nicest places— Antigua, Guatemala and then traveled farther south to the mountains of Peru, working in one of the remotest missions practicing my newly acquired language. One of the most uplifting aspects of my time in Peru was hiking up to Machu Picchu. As I was getting up close and personal with Nevada Salkantay, the iconic Andean peak and the most sacred mountain in the land of the Incas, I was visualizing what my second phase of sabbatical would look like. It was then the thought of writing a book captured my mind. I had always wanted to write something about my ministry. A good friend shared with me that writing—a book, short story, an individual life story, or poetry—is a goal for his time away from work. So, I embarked on a writing trajectory from day one of the second phase of my sabbatical. I immersed myself in my newly found freedom writing and reflecting while having lots of fun.

As I wrote this book on the Eucharist and the parts of the Mass, I was reminded of the story about a man who survived the Johnstown flood in Pennsylvania. He spent the rest of his life retelling his story of surviving that flood. He died and arrived in heaven and St. Peter met him at the gate and told him it was the custom for newcomers to address the heavenly host on their first night in residence. The man said, "No problem. I'll talk about my experience surviving the Johnstown flood." St. Peter replied, "Do what you like, but do remember that Noah will be in the audience."

As I mull over who my readers might be, I am acutely aware there will be many Noahs in the audience. Many of you have been in these waters much longer than I and have probably sailed much farther than I, and perhaps you are better equipped with knowledge and depth to steer readers through this important aspect of the Church's treasure. I hope you understand my quandary.

I ask for your prayers and blessings. I have served in a number of parishes in the Catholic Church and have been approached by individuals as well as groups, especially during parish retreats, to offer a talk or two on the parts of the Mass or do a 'teaching Mass.' I have had the joy of leading many groups to a deeper understanding of the Eucharist and helped many to appreciate the gift of God offered to us through the celebration of the Mass. And so, I embark on this mission with deep humility, accompanied by a sincere desire to reach out to those in our communities who yearn for a spiritually nourishing experience at Mass.

"I Am Making All Things New": The Christ Encounter

"There are many pious people who believe themselves to be saints who are not," wrote Tony Hendra, "and many people who believe themselves to be impious who are." According to him, a saint is a person who practices the keystone human virtue of humility—humility in the face of wealth and plenty, humility in the face of power and prestige, humility in the face of one's own genius or lack of it, humility in the face of love and beauty, and humility in the face of pain and death. God's chosen ones are driven to humbling themselves before the majesty and splendor of God and letting themselves be fashioned in a way that transcends our human understanding and expertise. A disciple is one who easily makes that transition from, "It's not about me," to "It's all about Him," and willingly embraces His will as one's own. A disciple is one who is deeply aware of personal inadequacies and unworthiness and recognizes God's greatness in attending to our lowliness in the mystery of the incarnation. The miracle and the mystery that surround the Eucharist and its celebration require of us an attitude of deep humility and openness to what God can do, when He enters our lives and our world through the Sacraments, especially the Eucharist.

One of my favorite gospel stories is the vocation narrative about Simon Peter. While being pressed in from all sides by the great crowd that had gathered on the shores of the Sea of Galilee, Jesus saw two boats on the shore. Peter and his partners had disembarked from their boats after a long night of fishing and were washing their nets. Jesus got into one of the boats and taught the crowd from a little distance. After he had finished talking, he asked Simon to put out into the deep and lower the nets for a catch. Simon responded, "Master, we have worked hard all night and have caught nothing, but at your command I will lower the nets" (Luke 5).

These words have profound implications for any apostle or minister. As a fisherman who spent his whole life in and around the Sea of Galilee, Peter had instinctive knowledge and understanding of the waters and the suitable timing for a catch. He and his partners had toiled the whole night combing through the vast lake without success, when the Lord solicited him to lower the nets. Peter's response is sincere and modest. "There are no fish around right now. We know these waters, and our expertise tells us that it is no use casting the nets." But then, Peter, humble and unassuming as he was, makes the transition from himself to the

Master, saying, "At your command, I will lower the nets."

In the life of Christians, there are times when they must transcend their expertise and knowledge and trust the Lord's words, even though it might seem to the naked eye a total failure or collapse. To leave our genius behind and follow a pedestrian order, to risk stepping out of a familiar present into an unfamiliar future, to leave security behind and opt instead for insecurity, to sell all we have and give it to the poor and follow the Master, to leave our boats behind and commit to an itinerant preacher, and the list goes on—all are indicative of a new paradigm in the mystery of God's call and action in the world. Faith is never against, but always above reason.

As we endeavor to unravel the mystery of God contained in the Eucharist, we must assume the mindset of an apostle like Peter, who responded to the Lord's request to put out into the deep and lower the net. "At your command, I will lower the nets." We prefer to stay in the shallows where it is safe. No riptide, no sharks, no storms that might turn our lives upside down. As we dive into the mystery of the Eucharist, I invite you to put yourself out deeper and then reach lower and trust the Lord, like Peter. Trust the Lord's Word. Trust his offer of eternal life. Trust that Jesus offers himself body and blood, soul, and divinity, as you put yourself into the deep with the Lord.

As Pope Francis reminds us, the heart of Christianity is found in the continuing encounter with the Lord, who has loved us, saved us, and laid down his life for us. There are three places to encounter the living Jesus. First, Jesus is alive and active in His Word. Second, we meet Him in the sacraments, especially in the breaking of the bread. Third, we meet Jesus in loving service to the least of our brothers and sisters.

The incredible truth is that the Eucharist encompasses all three encounters. In his apostolic letter, *On the Service of Charity*, Pope Benedict XVI expressed it best, "The Church's deepest nature is expressed in her threefold responsibility: of proclaiming the word of God (*kerygma-martyria*), celebrating the sacraments (*leitourgia*), and exercising the ministry of charity (*diakonia*). These duties presuppose each other and are inseparable."

The story of Simon Peter has only begun. When he followed the Lord's command and lowered his nets, he and his colleagues could not believe the catch of fish on that night, for their nets were tearing. When Simon Peter saw this, he fell at the knees of Jesus and said, "Depart from me, Lord, for I am a sinful man" (Luke 5: 8). Every encounter with the Lord opens our eyes to see ourselves as we truly are and to recognize the Lord as He truly is. That is the starting point for a life dedicated to holiness. Confronted with the splendor and majesty of God, Peter realized that he was just a man, a sinful man. Because of that, he became a humble man.

The following is a great quote: "The man who knows his own weakness is greater than the one who contemplates the angels." Peter would learn much more about himself and the Lord, and how much the Lord loved him, despite his weaknesses, in the many encounters that would follow. The transformation of Peter, the Galilean fisherman, to Leader of the Church is a story of multiple encounters with his Master and Lord, some of them painful, others reassuring, but all of them pedagogical and life-changing.

The Eucharist offers an encounter with the Risen Lord, who shares Himself with us through his Word and through sharing his most precious Body and Blood. The Lord will transform us, and our lives will never be the same. Like Peter, through our many encounters with the Lord in the Eucharist, we will unravel who we are and discover who God is.

These encounters with Jesus in the Eucharistic mystery contribute to our human and spiritual maturity. It is based on true transformation of the heart. Real encounter isn't just something religious method that we go through. The Eucharistic relationship isn't based just on head knowledge or lip service. It's having a real encounter with the Lord of Lord. There is a beautiful story in the book of

Isaiah that clearly validates what happens to a person that has an encounter with the Lord:

> In the year of King Uzziah's death I saw the Lord sitting on a throne, lofty and exalted, with the train of His robe filling the temple. Seraphim stood above Him, each having six wings: with two he covered his face, and with two he covered his feet, and with two he flew. And one called out to another and said, "Holy, Holy, Holy, is the Lord of hosts, The whole earth is full of His glory." And the foundations of the thresholds trembled at the voice of him who called out, while the temple was filling with smoke. Then I said, "Woe is me, for I am ruined! Because I am a man of unclean lips, and I live among a people of unclean lips; For my eyes have seen the King, the Lord of hosts." Then one of the seraphim flew to me with a burning coal in his hand, which he had taken from the altar with tongs. He touched my mouth *with it* and said, "Behold, this has touched your lips; and your iniquity is taken away and your sin is forgiven." Then I heard the voice of the Lord, saying, "Whom shall I send, and who will go for Us?" Then I said, "Here am I. Send me!" (Isaiah 6: 1-8).

In the midst of a terrifying encounter, Isaiah declares his unworthiness: "I am a man of unclean

lips, and I live among a people of unclean lips."
But God takes care of that: he dispatches one of the
seraphim with a live coal, and cleanses Isaiah's
lips forever, making him worthy to be a prophet,
God's own mouthpiece. If this sounds familiar, it is
because it is reminiscent of a pattern. It reminds us
of how God goes about the calling people. When
Jeremiah was called, he had an excuse, too --- he
was too young. "Ah Lord God," he cried, "I am
only a youth." But the Lord God reached out and
put words in his mouth. Amos protested that he
was only a shepherd and a tender of sycamore
trees; but the Lord told him to go and prophesy to
God's people anyhow.

Mary, when the Angel Gabriel visited her, was
incredulous at the thought of bearing the Christ
Child, but was assured that the Holy Spirit would
overshadow her. The truth of the divine encounters
is that if God calls, he provides. As Saint Augustine
said, "God does not choose a person who is worthy,
but by the act of choosing him he makes him
worthy." God does not call those who are fit, but he
fits those whom he calls. He empowers them with
strength to do what they are called to do. "I can do
all things through Him who strengthens me"
(Philippians 4: 13).

The same God who astounded Isaiah with his
perfection and glory also brought a coal from the
altar to touch Isaiah's lips, declaring him clean.
That coal had been drenched in the blood of a
sacrificial lamb, the only way that Isaiah was able to

stand before God's holiness. Every encounter with our Holy God sanctifies us, cleanses us and renders us capable of worthy worship. A Christ encounter can never leave us as we are but transformed and strengthened forever.

Cyril of Alexandria in the 400's said the coal in Isaiah 6 is unmistakably a picture of Christ, who, on our behalf, offered himself up to God the Father as a pure and unblemished sacrifice. "Let God then be on our lips like a glowing coal that burns away the rubbish of our sins, purges the filth of our unrighteousness, and sets us on fire with the Spirit" (*Isaiah: Interpreted by Early Christian Medieval Commentators* edited by Robert L. Wilken, Angela Russell Christman, Michael J. Hollerich page 83).

When the Lord touches our lips and tongues in the Eucharist, we are definitely in the midst of an encounter. The Second Vatican Council undertook a reform of the Church's liturgy. In its *Constitution on the Liturgy*, the Council Fathers wrote: "Mother Church earnestly desires that all the faithful should be led to that full, conscious, and active participation in liturgical celebrations, which is demanded by the very nature of the liturgy, and to which the Christian people, a chosen race, a royal priesthood, a holy nation, a redeemed people (I Peter 2:9, 4-5) have a right and obligation by reason of their baptism." Full and active participation in the liturgy is what each one of us is asked to engage in.

According to Bishop Paul S. Loverde, there are two important aspects when it comes to active participation. First, each one of us has a part in the liturgy, whether ordained or non-ordained. To exercise our ministerial or common priesthood effectively, we must understand what we are doing, consciously live out our priestly duties, and actively participate in the liturgical actions. Second, these actions are not individual actions. The celebration of the Eucharist is not a private devotion; rather, it is the public worship of God offered to the Father through Jesus Christ his Son in the unity of the Holy Spirit. Therefore, the gathered community should act in harmony, each carrying out their respective duties. In a homily on *Liturgical postures, gestures foster Unity, express reverence*, Bishop Loverde said:

> If members of the community do not act in union, but instead make the liturgy an expression of personal piety, then unity is turned into confusion, rhythm becomes chaos and the assembly is hindered from entering into the prayer of the liturgy and must rather focus on what is coming next. It is for this reason that the liturgical texts have rubrics. Rubrics are the authoritative rules and directions given to create order and harmony in the liturgy so that the People of God may enter into the prayer of the Mass. Because we are creatures of body and soul,

our prayer is not confined to our minds, hearts, and voices, but is expressed by our bodies as well.

It is my earnest hope and prayer that you too will be inspired to appreciate the gift of community and receive the gift of communion of mind and heart with one another and transition from individual or personal approach to the sacrament to communal participation.

Christians do not reckon as the world does, because Jesus has assigned a new meaning to what it takes to be truly human in our challenging world. Mother Teresa's daily encounter with the Lord in prayer, especially in the Eucharist, and the hours spent before the Blessed Sacrament, transformed her from a woman of the world to a woman dedicated to the service of the poorest of the poor. "Christian revolution is born in the liturgy," Pope Benedict preached in his homily on a Holy Thursday. And its "canon," its fundamental rule, is the great Eucharistic prayer. When the world is influenced by 'Eucharistic culture'—a culture of unconditional love, faithful service, and supreme sacrifice—we see the realization of "a new heaven and a new earth" as prophesied by St. John:

Then I saw a new heaven and a new earth; for the first heaven and the first earth passed away, and there is no longer *any* sea. And I saw the holy city, new Jerusalem, coming down out of heaven from God, made ready as a bride adorned for her husband. And I heard a loud voice from the throne, saying, "Behold, the tabernacle of God is among men, and He will dwell among them, and they shall be His people, and God Himself will be among them, and He will wipe away every tear from their eyes; and there will no longer be *any* death; there will no longer be *any* mourning, or crying, or pain; the first things have passed away." And He who sits on the throne said, "Behold, I am making all things new." And He said, "Write, for these words are faithful and true" (Rev 21: 1-5).

As Raymond E. Brown described, the new world to which Revelation witnessed is not created by imagination, but images serve as an entrée. To a world that accepts only what it can see, hear, and feel, these words point to what the eye has not seen, and the ear not heard. There is mystery and miracle in the Eucharist and no human imagination can truly conceive the majesty of life in the presence of God in the Eucharist and its transforming power on the world.

The Synod Fathers acknowledged this when they said: "Our Christian life, nourished by the Eucharist, gives us a glimpse of that new world— new heaven and new earth where the new Jerusalem come down from heaven, from God, "prepared as a bride adorned for her husband"

(*Sacramentum Caritatis*). John who wrote the book of Revelation and the words, "Behold, I am making all things new," also authored the Gospel of John in which he wrote, "The bread I will give is my flesh, for the life of the world" (John 6:51). The Eucharist is a sacrament of communion between brothers and sisters who allow themselves to be reconciled in Christ. Thus, the Lord bolsters our fraternal communion, and urges those in conflict to hasten their reconciliation by opening themselves to dialogue and a commitment to justice. In the words of the Synod Fathers, "The restoration of justice, reconciliation and forgiveness are the conditions for building true peace" and the establishment of the new Kingdom on earth (Sacramentum Caritatis).

Many Faces of the Eucharist

Ronald Rolheiser, OMI, in his essay, "The Many Faces of the Eucharist," lists a number of views held by the faithful about the Eucharist:

• For some it is a meal; for others, it is a sacrifice
• For some it is a ritual act, sacred and set apart; for others, it is a community gathering, the more mess and kids there are the better.
• For some it is a deep personal prayer; for others, it is a communal worship for the world.
• For some, its very essence is a coming together, a communion, of those united in a single denominational faith, while for others part of its essence is

its reaching out, its innate imperative to wash the feet of those who are different from ourselves.

• For some it is a celebration of sorrow, a making present of Christ's suffering and the place where we can break down; for others, it is the place to celebrate joy and sing alleluia.

• For some it is a ritual remembrance, a making present of the historical events of Jesus' dying, rising, ascending, and sending the Holy Spirit; for others, it is a celebration of God's presence with us today.

• For some it is a celebration of the Last Supper, something to be done less frequently, for others it is God's daily feeding of his people with a new manna, Christ's body, and is something to be done every day.

• For some it is a celebration of reconciliation, a ritual that forgives and unites, for others unity and reconciliation are pre-conditions for its proper celebration.

• For some it is a vigil act, a gathering that is essentially about waiting for something else or someone else to appear; for others, it is a celebration of something that is already present that is asking to be received and recognized

• For some it is understood to make present the real, physical body of Christ; for others it is understood to make Christ present in a real but spiritual way.

• Some call it the Lord's Supper, while others call it the Eucharist, or simply the Mass.

• Some celebrate it once a year, some four times a
year, some every Sunday, while others celebrate it
every day.

Rolheiser noted, "Who's right? In truth, the
Eucharist is all of these things and more. It is like a
finely cut diamond twirling in the sun, every turn
giving off a different sparkle. It is multivalent,
carrying different layers of meaning, some of them
in paradoxical tension with others. Even in
scripture, there is no one theology of the Eucharist,
Instead, there are various complementary
theologies of the Eucharist." According to Rolheiser, any attempt to nail down the full meaning
of the Eucharist will forever come up short,
because "it will eventually get up and walk away
with the nail."

According to *The Catechism of the Catholic Church*,
the different names we give to the Eucharist
express the inexhaustible richness of the Sacred
Mystery. Each name evokes a certain aspect of the
Mystery we celebrate. Today, the following terms
are used to describe different aspects of the
sacrament we celebrate.

• It is called **Eucharist**, because it is an action of
thanksgiving to God. The Greek words *eucharistein*
and *eulogein* recall the Jewish blessings that
proclaim—especially during a meal—God's works:
creation, redemption, and sanctification. This word

is more common among the members of the Catholic, Anglican and Episcopal Churches.

• The term, **The Lord's Supper**, is derived from the Last Supper the Lord shared with his disciples in the Upper Room, where he instituted the Eucharist, breaking bread and sharing the cup with them. This term is used directly in 1 Corinthians 11: 20 to describe this ceremony of remembrance.

• It is called **The Breaking of the Bread**, because Jesus used this rite, part of a Jewish meal, when as master of the table he blessed, broke and distributed the bread to the disciples during the Last Supper. It is by this action that his disciples would recognize him after his Resurrection, and it is this expression that the first Christians used to designate their Eucharistic assemblies.

• Some address it as the **Memorial of the Lord's Passion and Resurrection**, because it makes present here and now the one ultimate sacrifice of Jesus Christ on behalf of humanity and includes the Church's offering.

• The terms, **Holy Sacrifice of the Mass, Sacrifice of Praise, Spiritual Sacrifice**, and **Pure and Holy Sacrifice** are also used, since it completes and surpasses all the sacrifices of the Old Covenant.

• Some of the faithful and writers, especially in the Byzantine tradition—Western Orthodox, Oriental Orthodox, and some Eastern Rite Catholic Churches—view it as **The Holy and Divine Liturgy**, because the Church's whole liturgy finds its center and most intense expression in the celebration of this sacrament. In the same sense, we also call its celebration the **Sacred Mysteries**. The Church often speaks of the Most Blessed Sacrament, because it is the Sacrament of sacraments.

• Finally, **Holy Mass** (*Missa*), because the liturgy in which the mystery of salvation is accomplished concludes with the sending forth (*missio*) of the faithful to fulfill God's will in their daily lives.

Roman Catholics, as well as other denominations of Christians, have used this name. Regardless of how we address this Sacred Mystery, the most important aspect to remember is that it is a gift from God given our behalf, a gift of Himself. The Risen Lord comes to pitch His tent permanently in our midst. He has become the source and summit of our Christian lives. By using different names, we acknowledge that no single name can contain the inexhaustible wealth of meanings in this Sacred Mystery that we partake in.

Douglass M. Bailey narrated the following story. A couple with several young children visited the church where he was rector, seeking to become familiar with the Eucharist. In the Liturgy of that Sunday, when it was time for the congregation to come forward to the altar rail to receive the sacrament, their five-year-old son, sitting at the edge of the aisle, stage-whispered to his parents,

"Hurry Mom and Dad, let's go get some Christ!"
Yes! That is so powerful. Let us go and get some
Christ!

The Story of Emmaus

"They began to relate their experiences on the road and how He was recognized by them in the breaking of the bread" (Luke 24: 35).

One of the most telling encounters in the post-resurrection narratives is the Emmaus story. It forms the structure for the celebration of sacraments in the Church. The encounter between Jesus and the two disciples on the road to Emmaus unravels God's intervention in our human history through His Word and through the Sacrament. This encounter lends itself to the miracle of recognizing the Risen Lord who is alive and well, who walks with the believer in their anguish and sorrow. It is a story that reveals not only something about who the disciples were, but how Jesus opens their eyes of faith to see Him for who He truly is in a sacramental way through the breaking of the bread. This personal encounter mirrors what we Catholics celebrate in every sacrament. Jesus speaks to us in our human context through His Word, then transforms our lives through a miraculous pouring of inward grace, whereby we become the reality we celebrate and aspire for. In baptism, we become His mystical body; in marriage, the couple celebrate His mystical union; in Reconciliation, the penitent reunites his soul with God; in the Eucharist, the community receives the Word made Flesh; in priesthood, the candidate stands *in persona Christi*; in Anointing, the infirm share the Passion of Christ.

One of the first things the historical Jesus did was to gather together a band of disciples, whom He called apostles. They lived with him for three years, being schooled in a new and fuller understanding of who God is and how Jesus their Master is the anointed One of God. Everything came to an abrupt end, when Jesus was led to the cross and crucified as a criminal. The disciples were shattered. Some hovered behind closed doors for fear of the Jews, while others called it quits leaving town altogether, desiring to leave their past behind them in Jerusalem and search of a better future elsewhere.

The two disciples on the road to Emmaus represent the latter category. In spiritual pain, they realized that in stealing their Master and Guru from them, his enemies had also robbed them of their hope. Their future was now in their own hands. Everything about Jerusalem and its surroundings reminded them of their communion with Jesus. In their boundless sorrow, they embarked on a long and soulful journey, leaving behind a mystery that had given them hope and life.

The journey to Emmaus expounds the meaning

of the Sacraments more deeply. The two disciples probably argued and talked about events that they hoped would have had a different outcome. Deep in their hearts, they must have felt a sense of guilt and self-reproach for not standing with their arrested Master, who was tried, scourged, and put to death. They were overcome with sorrow and pain and could not see clearly. It was then that a stranger invited himself to walk with them, someone who seemed oblivious to the things that had just occurred. They shared with the stranger what was transpiring in their lives, how this man Jesus, who had instilled in them hope for a better life and freedom from oppression, was treated by the religious elders in collusion with the occupying Romans.

Jesus, who for now will remain a stranger, seemed to offer what the disciples had failed to connect and understand. He explained that everything that happened, no matter how dreadful and ghastly it might appear, was no accident, but willed by God. He quoted Scripture after Scripture, casting new light on the whole event. "Then beginning with Moses and all the prophets, he interpreted to them the things about himself in all the scriptures" (Luke 24: 27). The disciples began to see things in a different light. It was evening, but the they wanted to continue their conversation.

Their hearts burned within them as they heard the stranger explain the situation in a way they could never have imagined. His presence, his voice, His words gave them strength and hope. They invited him to dinner. Then, an amazing phenomenon took place. "When he was at the table with them, he took bread, blessed and broke it, and gave it to them. Then their eyes were opened, and they recognized him; and he vanished from their sight. They said to each other, 'Were not our hearts burning within us while he was talking to us on the road, while he was opening the scriptures to us?'" (Luke 24: 30-32).

Yes! Everything seemed so right. The Master's predictions were right. The women's story about Jesus being risen was true. The disciples could not contain their joy. They hurried back to the rest of the group to share what they had seen and heard, only to discover that Jesus was alive and well among their peers, as well.

This encounter between the Risen Lord and the distressed disciples models a believer's encounter in the Sacrament of the Eucharist. The stranger who walked, talked and argued with them was Jesus himself, hidden from their eyes and hearts, now through an inner strengthening of grace, truly appears to them as He truly is—the Risen Lord in their midst.

Let me draw attention to three important aspects of this story, as we endeavor to understand the celebration of the Eucharist.

1. Every Catholic comes to the celebration of the Mass with a human situation.

The disciples on the road to Emmaus were going through the most difficult and painful transitions in their life. The death of their Master and Lord had a debilitating effect on them. They were deeply grieving and did not know how to cope with their new life situation. They felt discouraged, confused and afraid. Their friends and colleagues hid behind closed doors for fear of the Jews. A mixture of confusion and fear filled the air. The two disciples in our story decided to leave town altogether. The longest and most painful walk one will ever undertake is away from the grave of someone you love. As Geoff Thomas put it:

To walk away and feel as if the world has come to an end. To walk away and think about what used to be, and what might have been. To walk away and realize, "I'll never be the same again." To play over and over in your mind the good times, the laughter, the fun stories, to reach out and touch a face and find it gone forever. To cry until you can't cry any more. To watch them bury your dreams and hopes and all that was good about life. To know it's over, done, finished, the end, and there is nothing you can do about it. To walk away to friends who cannot understand and to a world that cares little. It is the longest walk and the saddest day.

Every step takes you away from the tomb-
stone of a broken dream.

And Kathleen Ann Thompson asks:

Is there a tomb in your life that you've had to
walk away from? It doesn't have to be the
death of a loved one. It could be a relationship, a dream, a job you lost, or a disease
that left you unable to do the things you used
to do. After the shock wears off, take a step.
And another. You didn't choose the circumstances, but you can choose your response.
You can choose how to live this post-grave
life.

The disciples had walked from all of it—the
death of a loved one, a relationship, a dream, and a
job and, yes, from everything that mattered in their
lives. Down the road two people walked, crestfallen
and wanting to put the events of recent days behind
them. Jesus came to them unexpected and cast a
new light on their human situation.

We come to the Eucharistic celebration with our
own human situations. C.S Lewis stated, "God
doesn't want something from us, He simply wants
us." Some people believe we have to clean up our
lives before we come to the Lord. That is not the
case. Jesus speaks to the Samaritan woman at the
well, someone who lived in an illicit relationship
and who carried the baggage of five failed mar-

riages. In their encounter, Jesus addresses her situation and offers her salvation. To the woman caught in adultery, Jesus offers protection from the religious powers who concluded that she should be put to death. Instead, He offers forgiveness and mercy, sending her off saying, "Sin no more." Even to his disciples who had failed miserably, He offered love and compassion and grace upon grace to be restored to grace-fullness of discipleship.

Every personal encounter with Jesus presupposes a human need and a divine intervention of love, forgiveness, and grace. "The most important thing that can happen to a person," Pope Francis explained in a homily, "is to encounter Jesus, who loves us, who has saved us, who gave his life for us." Further, he explained that we encounter Jesus in three ways. Jesus is alive in His Word. We meet Jesus in the sacraments, especially in regular participation in the Eucharist and the sacrament of reconciliation. And third, we meet Jesus in our loving service to those in need, those who live on the periphery of society.

"Are you struggling with something in your life?" asks Bishop Bartholomew Manjoro. Are you troubled by the way your life is going? Are you suffering because of what people are thinking and talking about you? You need to have a divine encounter. This encounter, according to the bishop comes with deep revelations of secrets hidden and the breaking of curses.

One powerful divine encounter that has always impressed me took place after the resurrection. "Simon Peter and Thomas, called Didymus, and Nathanael of Cana in Galilee, and the *sons* of Zebedee, and two others of His disciples were together. Simon Peter said to them, 'I am going fishing.' They said to him, 'We will also come with you.' They went out and got into the boat; and that night they caught nothing" (John 21: 1-3).

Let's focus for a moment on the statement made by Peter. "I'm going fishing." Is this recreational fishing? Or is Peter so bored that he thinks, *I feel like going fishing.* Peter had spent the last three years of his life following Jesus, doing what Jesus asked him to do. Now, Jesus isn't there anymore to be followed. Peter senses failure. He has failed the Lord. He has failed Jesus. He has not just failed at some task or other, but in his discipleship. He has let Jesus down. Remember Peter's bold statement to Jesus in the full hearing of his colleagues: "Even though all may fall away because of You, I will never fall away" Mathew (26: 33). Peter had catastrophically let Jesus down after promising and bragging that he would be there. He could not bring himself to the thought that he would ever be useful in the ministry of 'catching men.' I believe this is the heart of Peter's statement. "I'm going back to fishing"—back to what I'm good at, to what I know, fishing.

Scholars are divided on this interpretation, but

to me Peter was saying, "To heck with it. My job as a disciple is over. I'm going back to my old life as a fisherman." Peter was just as discouraged and dejected as the two disciples on the road to Emmaus. He decided to go back to normal—the apparent security of his old way of life as a fisherman on the Sea of Galilee. Let bygones be bygones. I am moving on. I am going fishing. The other disciples said, "We will also come with you."

Remember Murphy's Law? "Anything that can go wrong, will go wrong, at the worst possible time, all the time, without fail, when you least expect it?" That night, Peter and his crew spent the whole night fishing and caught nothing. If discouragement and dejection don't get you, failure will start to haunt your spirit. It hits you hard. I'm not good enough. I'm such a failure. I'm a loser. But God thinks about you differently. You are not a failure. You are not a loser. The divine encounter that follows changes everything:

> But when the day was now breaking, Jesus stood on the beach; yet the disciples did not know that it was Jesus. So, Jesus said to them, "Children, you do not have any fish, do you?"
> They answered Him, "No."
> And He said to them, "Cast the net on the right-hand side of the boat and you will find *a catch*."

So, they cast, and then they were not able to haul it in because of the great number of fishes. Therefore, that disciple whom Jesus loved said to Peter, "It is the Lord." When Simon Peter heard that it was the Lord, he put his outer garment on (for he was stripped *for work*) and threw himself into the sea. But the other disciples came in the little boat, for they were not far from the land, but about one hundred yards away, dragging the net *full* of fish. So, when they got out on the land, they saw a charcoal fire *already* laid and fish placed on it, and bread (John 21: 4–9).

Jesus meets Peter on the shore. He is acutely aware of his inadequacies as a man, as a disciple, and the sense that failure has crippled his heart and mind. Addressing Peter and his friends as "Children," He asks Peter to drop the net for a catch. No matter how you feel, no matter how low you have plunged as a human being, you are still and will always be 'God's child.' And He loves you just like before. Peter dropped the net and the catch was unbelievable. It is the Lord! He is alive. Jesus has prepared a meal for them on the shore. At the table fellowship, Peter is reoriented and invited into a reunion. Peter is fully restored to relationship. In three different ways, Jesus asks Peter to reaffirm his love for Him: "Simon, son of John, do you love Me more than these?" (John 21: 15, 16, and 17). Why? Because he had denied Him three times. Peter's response each time is consistent and sincere: "Lord, you know all things; you know that I love you." The response of Jesus each time, "Tend my sheep. Feed my lambs," stamps Peter's calling to be an apostle. Peter will lead the Church as Christ asked him to. And, he will lay down his life in the footsteps of his Master.

Are you struggling with something in your life? Are you troubled by the way your life is going? Are you suffering because of what people might think and say about you? You need a divine encounter.

One of the most poignant examples of such an encounter is the one that transformed an enemy of God into a warrior on his behalf. Saul was a persecutor of the early Church. Christians dreaded the very thought of this mighty colossus, who was an enemy of Jesus. He believed in God and thought he was doing God a favor by dragging men and women who believed in Jesus into prison. One day everything changed. Saul was struck.

Bishop Bartholomew described it as an accident, a divine accident. When he felt the impact of this divine encounter, he fell from his horseback. Suddenly a light shone around him that seemed like a flash of lightening. It blinded him and rendered him helpless. He who once rode like a mighty Colossus now had to lick dust. God had taken over. He heard a voice from heaven, "'Saul, Saul, why are you persecuting Me?' And he said, 'Who are You, Lord?' And He said, 'I am Jesus whom you are persecuting, but get up and enter the

city, and it will be told you what you must do'"
(Acts 9: 3-5).

Saul did not have to be told who it was that
appeared to him, for he knew immediately in his
heart. God had revealed himself to this man, who
considered himself a sworn enemy of Jesus, set on
a mission to annihilate Christians. He now became
a true disciple of Jesus. In the words of Alex
Rebello, in *Broken Stillness*, "When Saul lost his
sight, he found his vision." When reduced to
no-thing, Saul let God became everything. it was
when he became powerless that God became
powerful. Only when he fell, emptied, into God's
hands could God fill him with supporting and
sustaining grace, converting him into a vessel of
election.

In celebrating the Eucharist, the disciple
encounters the Lord just as she or he is, believing
that God will indeed offer welcome. The redeeming grace of the sacrament will sanctify a life
standing in dire need. Everything begins with
human need. To be in His sacred ground with a
heart aware of deep spiritual need is a prerequisite
to the celebration of the Eucharist. Though you
may feel hopeless, God is ready to offer you hope.
Are you hurt and angry? God wants to heal your
hidden wounds. Do you feel empty and
meaningless? God wants to fill your life with
purpose and joy. To sit in the pew in deep prayer
and reflection, confronting our demons, our
wretchedness, our lack of joy and peace, our bro-

ken relationships forms the ground on which Jesus meets us in a personal and deeply spiritual encounter through His Word and through the breaking of the bread. Like the publican who stood at a distance deeply aware of his wretchedness, you stake your hopes and claims, not on anything you have done or deserve, but entirely on the mercy of God.

This can start even before you leave for church. Just as Jesus encountered the disciples on the road of anguish and despair, Jesus encounters you on the road of despair and helplessness. You come as you are; you open your heart to him and believe that, in the hour that follows, God will enter into your life in a way that you have never known. He will cast new light on your life situation. You will recognize Him as He truly is. And, like the disciples, you will return to your home, to your work, to your relationships, with renewed mind and heart. *He is alive. I am back.*

One of the beautiful Advent expressions comes from Prophet Isaiah, who foretold, "A shoot shall sprout from the stump of Jesse" (Isaiah 11: 1). A stump is what was formerly a living, thriving tree. But the tree no longer lives or thrives. Perhaps it was cut down or died and fell over. All you see today is the stump, the wood of death. Our lives are, at times, defined in terms of stumps. The world of the disciples on the road to Emmaus seemed like a dead stump, made desolate by the sudden and ignominious death of their Master. Sitting in the pews, these dead situations are what some of us might be dealing with right now—a crumbling relationship, demons in our lives like drugs, lust, jealousy, bitterness, our families, and neighborhoods devastated by violence and poverty or fear of the unknown. The world perceives these situations as dead and lost forever. When we open our eyes in faith, illumined by God's Word and nourished by eternal food, these same things are just seed ground for the new shoot to sprout. God can bring forth new life from the grave where there is only decay or rottenness. That is the power of the Sacraments. That is the power of the Risen Lord walking with us in our anguish and hopelessness.

2. Encountering Jesus in His Word.

The road to Emmaus is built solidly on Sacred Scripture. Jesus speaks directly to the crestfallen disciples. "Then beginning with Moses and all the prophets, he interpreted to them the things about himself in all the scriptures" (Luke 24: 27). It is no wonder that every sacrament commences with celebration of God's Word, because it illumines our minds and lights up our darkness. "And they said one to another, 'Did not our hearts burn within us, while he talked with us on the way, and while he opened to us the scriptures?" This expression emphasizes the deepest interest and pleasure which the disciples experienced as they listened to Scripture in the context of their life situation. Through Sacred Scripture, the stranger had convincingly shown them that the Messiah had to suffer and die, that the world might be saved. The encounter with His Word leads them to recognize Jesus himself as He truly is. Their lives had changed forever. Illumined by God's Word, enlightened by the light of his Word in their darkness, the disciples now recognize Him in the breaking of the bread.

That is what the Word of God can do to you. Celebration of Sacred Scripture in the Eucharist opens your eyes of faith, and you recognize Him in the breaking of the bread. That which is hidden from you now unravels as the true gift in its beauty and grandeur. Only when His Word shed a light on their human condition did they perceive as they never had before. Celebrating God's Word is a precursor to the Eucharistic miracle. It illumines, it enlightens and prods you to open your eyes to the Eucharistic miracle. "Their eyes were opened, and they recognized him."

The tragedy of modern times is that we have lost our gift of attention. In her classic, "The Mocking-birds," Mary Oliver talks about an impoverished couple who opened their doors to strangers and had nothing to give except their willingness to be attentive. The strangers turned out to be gods. For this alone the gods loved them, says Mary Oliver, and they blessed them when they rose out of their mortal bodies. "Like a million particles of water from a fountain, the light swept into all the corners of the cottage, and the old couple, shaken with understanding, bowed down." The finest gift we humans can offer today to God is the gift of our attention. When we listen attentively, God lights up all the corners of our lives, and a new understanding takes over our hearts and minds.

During the celebration of the Eucharist, it comes with two-fold graces. First, God's Word casts a new light on our human conditions and our need. We see where our lives are directed even in our darkness. Second, it opens our eyes of faith to witness the miracle that the sacrament embodies—the bread becomes body, wine becomes blood, and we become sharers and partakers of the one ultimate sacrifice.

3. They got up and retuned to Jerusalem.

The disciples could not wait. How could they? They returned to Jerusalem, the place that had apparently annihilated their hopes and dreams. It is their new understanding of reality, illumined and enlightened by the Word of God that has propelled them back to a place and state from which they once fled. They knew they had to go back and live the new reality, because it was just as God had planned. They reunited with the rest of the group only to learn that they, too, had seen and experienced the Risen Lord.

The Emmaus story reveals three loves spread across the act, which today is translated into three kisses during the Mass—kiss of Scripture (Liturgy of the Word), kiss of the Altar (Liturgy of the Eucharist) and the kiss of Peace (Liturgy of Service).

It denotes three integral parts of the Mass, without which a fuller celebration is not possible. The stranger, the Word of God and the breaking of the bread constitute the essentials of the story. The disciples welcomed the stranger, opened their hearts to him and He joined in fellowship with them. At the celebration of the Eucharist, we welcome the stranger, join in fellowship, and seal our love with a kiss of peace. The communion we share with Jesus is fully celebrated in our communion with the entire community, with whom we whom we only share love and peace. We will address the kiss of Scripture and the kiss of the Altar in depth in the following chapters. And then, I would draw your attention to the kiss of Peace— the kiss of the stranger—which defines our lives after the Eucharistic meal in terms of "body that is broken, broken for the world."

I would like to address hospitality as related to the Eucharistic celebration. How do we receive newcomers or newly returned members with a genuine spirit of welcome that provides them a bridge to cross from the worldly culture to the Eucharistic culture?

Welcoming the Stranger
and Eucharistic Hospitality

Let no one ever come to you without leaving better and happier. Be the living expression of God's kindness: kindness in your face, kindness in your eyes, kindness in your smile (Mother Teresa).

One of the central aspects of the Mass for those who participate is the Kiss of Peace—the kiss of the stranger before, during, and after Mass, because the Eucharist is a never-ending mystery that translates itself in our own transformation and change. It is impossible to confine God to just one hour, because He lives on in the person of the sharer or partaker of the mystery. The first Christian community was indeed a Eucharistic community, defined by the love and concern they had for one another. "See how they love one another."

Division, discrimination, racism, indifference, poverty, and steep individualism, all of these run counter to what Eucharist represents and symbolizes—communion of mind and heart. Eucharist strengthens us to love the unlovable, to touch the untouchable, to receive the unacceptable and share God-given gifts with those in deep need. Mother

Teresa built her congregation centered on the Eucharist. Her nuns broke bread together, Eucharist, every day. Then spent a couple of hours before the Blessed Sacrament during the day and took prayer breaks during work. One story has been repeated many times. A reporter watched Mother Teresa as she cleaned the maggot-infested wound of a man on the street. He told Mother, "I would not do what you do for a million dollars." Mother replied with a smile, "I wouldn't either." The truth is that she and her nuns recognized the face of Christ in the poor, disfigured, marginalized and the abandoned. Touching the Eucharistic Lord at the Mass was no different from touching the face of Jesus in the poorest of the poor with whom Jesus so often identified himself. "I see God in every human being. When I wash the leper's wounds, I feel I am nursing the Lord himself. Is it not a beautiful experience?" (Mother Teresa).

In a blog post, "Welcoming the stranger and recognizing the divine in our midst," Terry Biddington states, "Creation reveals that all difference, otherness and strangeness originate in God and that God is, therefore, inherently open to difference in all its forms." The mystery of our God is that He manifests Himself in ways and forms that we least expect. In the incarnation, God revealed Himself to mankind in the helpless little Child of Bethlehem, around whom the angels and shepherds gathered in prayer and worship, to whom Kings from the East brought gifts of gold, myrrh and frankincense. The Kingdom of Egypt welcomed God in their midst as a refugee, fleeing from the wrath and insecurity of Herod. To the disciples on the road to Emmaus, God was a stranger who invited himself into their company as they journeyed in anguish and sorrow to a strange land, where they wanted to start their lives all over again. "I was a stranger and you welcomed me," is how Jesus addressed himself in Mathew 25.

According to Biddington, we humans all too often shy nervously away from what is different and 'other,' including the strange otherness of God's own presence. In doing so, we limit ourselves to operating within the confines of sameness and familiarity.

What is amazing about our God is that it is about us. We are made in the image and likeness of a God who encompasses all difference; a God is who is a community of three persons. Let me draw a few applications. Diversity, communion they are inherently God attributes. People of diverse cultural backgrounds are God's gifts. What leads people to associate with those who are similar, while distancing themselves from diverse others? What causes us to categorize other groups in distorted ways? What gives rise to racism, discrimination in our hearts, in our communities? For sure, it does not come from our God. It is not an expression of our faith. I believe the primary motive that drives the church to embrace ethnic diversity, inclusiveness and outreach is the conviction that all of these are intrinsic God-values. And God manifests Himself in ways and forms we least expect.

One of the first miracles of the New Testament Church is the miracle of inclusion and outreach. After Pentecost, the apostles were filled with the Holy Spirit and began to speak in different tongues. As they proclaimed the Word of God on the streets of Jerusalem, the diverse crowd gathered together to listen to the apostles was astounded and amazed, because each one heard them speaking in his own language.

> Are not all these people who are speaking Galileans? Then how does each of us hear them in his own native language? We are Parthians, Medes, and Elamites, inhabitants of Mesopotamia, Judea and Cappadocia, Pontus and Asia, Phrygia and Pamphylia, Egypt and the districts of Libya near Cyrene, as well as travelers from Rome, both Jews and converts to Judaism, Cretans and Arabs, yet we hear them speaking in our own tongues of the mighty acts of God." They were all astounded and bewildered, and said to one another, "What does this mean?" (Acts 2: 7-12)

As the Christian community gathers together at the Eucharist, regardless of their differences, God's inclusive Spirit makes it possible for them not only to understand one another in the Spirit, but also to hear God's Word in a way that is familiar and easy: "Each one heard them speaking in his own language." Eucharistic hospitality graces us in His Spirit as we listen to His Word, opening our eyes of faith. It then enables us to recognize Jesus in the breaking of the Bread. God expressed the gift of inclusion and out-reach across difference in the out-pouring of the Spirit in the Eucharistic celebration, which transforms the lives of the people joined together in communities. The Spirit of God, invoked in the Eucharistic prayer (Epiclesis), breaks open structures that confine and separate people, so they can welcome difference and otherness, which is unique to God himself. We become one body, one spirit in Jesus.

Eucharistic hospitality encompasses more than what is necessarily offered at the vestibule of the Church by cheerful and welcoming ushers and greeters. It transcends coffee and doughnuts, provided after Mass. While these are important aspects of our communion and fellowship, Eucharistic hospitality is a two-fold reality: God's offer of grace and welcome and eternal hospitality at the Table of the Word and the Altar. Scriptures testify to the truth that grace and invitation of God precede any human response of faith and love of God. Jesus asked the Samaritan woman at the well, who had married five times and was now in an irregular relationship, for hospitality in the request for a drink of water. He then offered her eternal hospitality: "But whoever drinks of the water that I will give him shall never thirst; but the water that I will give him will become in him a well of water springing up to eternal life" (John 4: 14).

A sinful woman walked into a room full of self-righteous men and washed the feet of Jesus with her tears and dried them with her hair. She then anointed him with a perfume of immense value. It was a profound and grateful gesture of hospitality symbolic of the grace of eternal salvation afforded to her earlier.

To Zacchaeus, a man despised and considered an outcast in religious circles and his immediate neighborhood, Jesus offered hospitality when he said to the man perched on a tree limb: "Zacchaeus! Quick, come down! I must be a guest in your home today" (Luke 19:5). This radical love broke through division, hatred, loneliness, shame, and greed and revealed God's inclusive love and outreach. He crossed 'taboo' boundaries and triggered offense by his open welcome.

At the Last Supper, Jesus washed the feet of his disciples as a lesson in service and an invitation to share in His Divine Life, then broke bread and poured wine in anticipation of the ultimate sacrifice He would offer on behalf of humanity. In this sense, it behooves us to welcome all who seek God in Christ, inviting them to experience the grace and salvation that stem from the Eucharist, before insisting upon a faith commitment. The parables of Jesus emphasize this dimension of Jesus reaching out to sinners, sparked by nothing at all from those who have strayed from his love, rather purely from his deep desire to save the lost. And upon finding the lost, there is no immediate rebuke; rather what comes next is calling together friends and neighbors to celebrate. "When Jesus ate with those whom others shunned, he modeled a ministry that was redemptive and revelatory," writes professor Joseph Galgalo. It is about receiving, welcoming and integrating the lost ones into communion with others with joy and festivity. Eucharistic hospitality, then, can be defined in terms of welcoming the stranger and the lost, then integrating them into the community.

During his lifetime, Jesus' offer of hospitality and welcome, inclusion and outreach set the stage for one of his most profound and nonnegotiable teachings on the 'Bread of Life' and the institution of the Eucharist. The feeding of the 5,000 appears in all the Gospels, with slight variations, and stands out as an extraordinary model of hospitality that precludes any consideration of conditions as prerequisites. This is characteristic of any act of hospitality offered by Jesus. In the miraculous feeding, Jesus set the stage for the discourse on the Bread of Life, that He is the bread of life (John 6).

In the words of Jason Foster, "Jesus the Host provides tangible bread to feed the stomachs of the people, but this bread also points to an even greater sense of Jesus as Host—that He is the very bread of life who eternally feeds His people and they do not

perish." During the Last Supper, He washed the
feet of all the disciples, including Judas, knowing
full well that he was en route to the greatest act of
betrayal. In lowering himself as a slave, washing
the feet of His disciples, even the one whose heart
was astray, he set the stage for the institution of the
Eucharist. Thus, even today Christian hospitality is
the grid through which we communicate God to the
strangers in our midst. I would like to draw the
following principal arguments based on this discussion:

1. Christian hospitality is offered to everyone
regardless of a person's spiritual condition or
disposition. "Do not neglect to show hospitality to
strangers, for by this some have entertained angels
without knowing it" (Hebrews 13: 2).
2. Christian Hospitality should set the stage for
formation of intentional disciples through teaching
and witnessing. In this sense, Christian hospitality
is a Sacred Process of receiving outsiders and transforming them from strangers to disciples. It is about
integration. "The Church must integrate, not
exclude, Catholics in irregular situations" (Pope
Francis).
3. Christian spirituality precedes Eucharistic hospitality. Jesus the host feeds us with His own Body
and Blood. It is our responsibility to create the
ambiance of openness and trust, whereby God
initiates the process of grace and change. Dr. Paul
A. Lance said, "Hospitality is our work and our

witness long before telling anyone what we believe. A warm welcome, and a ready spirit of assistance (whoever they are, wherever they are along life's journey) must be in evidence before we can expect anyone to trust us with their personal story, let alone with the care of their spiritual lives!"

The ministry of ushers and greeters facilitates this aspect of hospitality. It must be practiced by the congregation in the pews, in the aisles, inside and outside the Church. Lance further noted that a living, lasting faith in God is not based on the content of a sermon, but on conversations between real people. Yes! It is not so much what we sing or say or do in Church, but what we say and do outside the Sacred Enclosure that "weaves our lives together with the warp and woof of true Christianity." Our smiles and words of welcome must turn into conversations, eventually around shared meals in our homes or in the Church facilities to which we welcome newcomers or those newly returned. These are the kinds of experiences that help build integration and promote our care and love for one another as a community.

Through his incarnation, Jesus entered into our strange and hostile world to communicate to us Who God is and offer us salvation. In Christian hospitality, we enter into the world of others in an effort to understand them, to be a friend to them, and witness to them. Hospitality, according to James Foster is the flip side of the Incarnation. "Hospitality is the act of inviting other people into our world, in order to accomplish the same things. When we invite our neighbors to Church, we are asking them to enter our world in the hope of that they might discover Jesus and their need for a Savior and become part of the Christian family of the forgiven."

The wonder and the scandal of the incarnation is that God not only dwelt among us unworthy people, but that he also called all of us, without exception, into the mystery of His love. Our Christian hospitality, modeled on God's own great hospitality in the incarnate Word, should assist Churches and their leadership into considering how wide they have flung open the doors of their Churches and how much more they must do to all whom God may be leading there. On October 22, 1978, Pope John Paul II began his pontificate with the words: "Do not be afraid, I say open wide the doors for Christ." And Christ is identified in the hungry, thirsty, or ill, and those in prison or otherwise in need of redemption.

In a homily directed towards welcoming all people in our Churches, in the context of the Scripture passage that described the Pharisees as laying obstacles, Pope Francis said: 'Today's mildly rebuked Pharisees are the self-appointed pastoral border guards who hold up a hand in consternation, instead of offering one in welcome when the less-than-perfect among us seek to gate crash at the house of the Lord." Pope Francis warned, 'There is always a temptation to try to take possession of the Lord." The pope spoke of an unofficial '8th' sacrament created by parish gatekeepers to throw up obstacles to those they deem unworthy.

Formation is the key component of Eucharistic hospitality, one which is shaped by the needs, personal history and understanding of the stranger or those in irregular situations. There is no 'one size fits all' approach that we often tend to demand of our people. Eucharistic hospitality means that every member is a faithful and welcoming host, adept with understanding and knowledge to reach out and bring the newcomer into the fold without the rigidity and inflexibility that is often the mark of some of our communities.

In the Acts of the Apostles, Paul who was not only a stranger, but a sworn enemy of the Christian people, is taken in by the disciples and offered hospitality. That gift transforms him from being an enemy to a guest, and eventually to a witness. God addressed the fears of Ananias about Paul and his malicious intentions to murder Christians, asking him to reach out to him in prayer, because God had chosen him as His instrument to spread the Gospel among the Gentiles.

Acts 9:23 says, "After many days had gone by . . . ." Commentators connect that elusive phrase with Paul's statement in Galatians 1:17 that, right after his conversion, he "went away to Arabia and returned once more to Damascus." Scripture is unclear about how long he was in Arabia, but Paul says: "When God, who had set me apart even from my mother's womb and called me through His grace, was pleased to reveal His Son in me so that I might preach Him among the Gentiles, I did not immediately consult with flesh and blood" (Gal. 1:15-16). The expression "I did not immediately consult with flesh and blood" indicates that he went there to hear directly from God and allow God to rearrange his theology. He was in prayer and retreat, deciphering God's will and His mission for him.

In Acts, Chapter 9, we see the next stage of Paul's formation in Jerusalem with Barnabas, a well-known leader and teacher as his advocate. Later on, Paul is teamed with Barnabas in Antioch and together they met with the Church and taught a great number of people (Acts 11: 26). It was in Antioch, nine years after his conversion, that Paul's launched his ministry as a spiritual leader and apostle. To the church that once dreaded Saul, the ringleader of the movement to exterminate Christianity, he turned out to be a friend, a fellow-believer, in fact, a vigorous evangelist, who proclaimed Christ more clearly and powerfully than anyone had previously done. The church did not shrink or suffer for Saul's arrival. It grew because of it.

As God asked Ananias to cast aside legitimate fears about an enemy he had led to the doors of the early Church, congregations today must be willing to let go of our fears and uncertainties with regard to the stranger. It is God who leads them to our doors. Spiritual formation of our newcomers, as well as the older ones, must include helping them to learn how to study God's Word and teach them how to pray. There is no shortcut when it comes to helping someone to be an intentional disciple and preparing them to accept God's hospitality in the Eucharist.

It takes courage and strength to move from 'Disney hospitality,' offered at our churches, to Christian and Eucharistic hospitality, which is an imitation of Christ, the Incarnate Word who entered into our world and our lives. We spend so much time and energy training greeters and ushers, creating nametags, and percolating coffee, that we forget about the real needs of the person who stands before us. As Arthur Sullivan explains:

"In the light of Jesus' life, death, resurrection, and return, Christian hospitality is the intentional, responsible, and caring act of welcoming or visiting, in either public or private places, those who are strangers, enemies, or distressed, without regard for reciprocation.

Jesus intentionally entered the shattered lives of the disciples on the road to Emmaus, and in the privacy of their journey reached out to their problems. Their hearts were burning as He spoke to them and explained the Scriptures. He moved them from fugitives to intentional disciples, ready to take on the world as it unraveled before them. They went back and joined the community of the disciples and spent many days in prayer and study with them, awaiting the outpouring of the Holy Spirit. We can define Eucharistic hospitality, then, in terms of integrating the stranger. No longer feeling estranged in our midst, they become active members who feel loved and nurtured by the community.

During my 1999 visit to Geneva, Switzerland, my host family, who were not Catholics, first took me to a Catholic Church for Mass on Sunday. Then they invited me to join them at an ecumenical service conducted by their Church. In a 100 percent white Church, I was the only one person of color, and they welcomed me with joy. I was at home as I sat down in the pew with a community I had never met or seen. They surprised me during communion. The entire congregation moved from their seats and formed in a circle along the walls of the Church for communion. I stood with them in a corner. The Ministers walked up to me first with bread and wine, as if I was a special guest in that gathering. They smiled and gave me communion. As one of the ministers shared the cup, she said, "We are so happy you are with us." Of course, I was overjoyed and thanked my hosts for the uplifting experience at their Church.

I have reflected on that experience multiple times and have desired to bring such awesome hospitality to my own Church. Having said that, I

have been bothered by another deeper understanding of Eucharistic hospitality. The shared meal
is not merely a social act of friendship, but more a
religious act of fellowship and communion with
God and one another. Beyond the feeling of
inclusion and welcome, expressed in a shared meal,
what I missed most was the true intimacy that
comes from receiving Jesus' body and Blood.
Welcoming the strangers in our midst is the first
step in the process of integrating them in the
community and preparing them to be graced by
Eucharistic hospitality. Jesus comes in His body
and Blood and transforms them into oneness with
Him, which is of greater significance.

Holy Communion is not magic, rather one's
disposition and understanding of the Sacred
Mystery changes everything in the communicant.
God gives life. That life is rooted in His image and
likeness. Receiving Jesus in communion helps to
bring out all those characteristics of the divine
essence deep within the core of who we are and
what we are meant to be—children of God. To lead
our visitors and friends through such spiritual
experience and growth, Eucharistic hospitality
requires the Church to form them into disciples, as
Jesus formed the disciples on the road to Emmaus,
in the light of the Scriptures and prayer.

There is serious debate right now in our Church
regarding Eucharistic hospitality in terms of who
can and should not receive communion. It stems
from debates in the Synod of Bishops regarding the

possibility of divorced and remarried Catholics receiving Holy Communion. This is a healthy debate for many reasons. On the one hand, it leads insiders to understand and appreciate the gift of the most precious Body and Blood of Jesus in a deeper way, while embracing an attitude of humility and gratefulness. We must take to heart the teaching of our Holy Father Pope Francis who stated, "Eucharist is not a prize for the perfect, but a powerful medicine and nourishment for the weak."

In the words of Thomas D. Williams, "The Eucharist is no gold star on the forehead of 'good' Christians, but an undeserved gift to strengthen pilgrims who stumble along through life with their gaze fixed on heaven."

On the other hand, there is much that we have to offer the outsiders in terms of Christian hospitality before affording Eucharistic hospitality. Like the Father who rushed to meet his prodigal son and offered him hospitality that included new clothes and a ring on his finger, so he could be one with the family and celebrate the feast of the fatted calf, we must rush to meet the newly arrived in our own churches, or the newly returned, meeting their immediate needs and providing for their spiritual needs, so they can fully celebrate the feast of the Lamb as a full-fledged member of the Catholic family.

There is a relationship between mercy and justice and between charity and truth. The question is how the Church can live these seemingly opposing principles in the real world. The discussion afoot in the Church should lead us to take a step backwards to examine the fundamental understanding of the Catholic Church about what it means to receive Holy Communion, and how it leads to spiritual growth and holiness in the recipient. Such an understanding will surely change the tone of today's demand for Eucharistic hospitality.

Outreach and inclusion were the characteristic marks of the historical Jesus, who welcomed sinners and shared table fellowship with them. Ronald Rolheiser writes, "True orthodoxy asks us to hold a great tension, between real boundaries beyond which you may not go and real borders and frontiers to which you must go. You may not go too far, but you must also go far enough. . . . There is danger in bad dogma but there is equal danger in not radiating, with sufficient compassion and understanding, God's universal will for the salvation of all peoples."

I believe that an attitude of openness to charity and truth is at the heart of the celebration of the Eucharist.

Jesus invites everyone to the Eucharistic Table. Ian G. Barbour, in *Wholeness in Science and Personal Life* wrote, "If you know the brokenness of life, its fractures within and its division without, then you have participated in the broken body of Christ, and you are invited to share in the breaking of the bread. If you desire to know the love of God that overcomes indifference and despair, if you desire the reconciliation that overcomes estrangement and alienation, then you are invited to share the cup of the new covenant."

At the Last Supper, Jesus surrounded himself with a group of unfocused apostles whose hearts were far from perfect. It is in offering hospitality to a stranger that the disciples come to experience God and recognize him in the breaking of the bread. Eucharist annihilates barriers between people, destroys racism at its roots, and ushers in the Messianic era of peace and prosperity for everyone of good will. As the prophets of old foretold, the wolf and the lamb shall lie together. In the New Covenant in His Blood, Jesus will bring together people of every race and tongue.

There is an intimate and rich relationship between Eucharistic communion and ecclesial communion, which makes it generally impossible for non-Catholic Christians to receive the former without enjoying the latter. There is one Church because there is one Christ. It's an ancient concept called "Christus Totus," Latin for "the whole Christ." It means that Christ comprises Christ and the Church, head and members, head and body. Christ is us and we are Christ. Indeed, if on the one hand Eucharistic communion unites us more fully to the Christus totus, Head and members, it requires, on the other, that this communion already exist (Sacramentum Caritatis).

Preparing for Mass

"He will show you a large room upstairs, furnished and ready. Make preparation for us there" Mark 14:15.

A little girl, dressed in her Sunday best, was running as fast as she could, trying not to be late for Bible class. As she ran she prayed, "Dear Lord, please don't let me be late! Dear Lord, please don't let me be late!" While running and praying, she tripped on a curb and fell, getting dirty and tearing her dress. She got up, brushed herself off, and started running again. As she ran she once again began to pray, "Dear Lord, please don't let me be late. . . . But please don't shove me either!"

Have you ever been late to a ceremony? Did you feel ashamed or uncomfortable as you walked in after everyone was seated and the function had begun? I had a friend who missed his flight because he was late. So, the airlines rescheduled his flight for the evening. He went downtown to meet a friend and missed that flight too. So, they put him on a flight for the following morning. He got up late and missed that too. He called me up distressed and upset. I told him he needed help.

Faithful parishioners have asked me, "How much Mass must you miss to miss Mass?" I have joked with friends saying, "As long as you arrive before the collection, you are good." There is so much more to the mystery of the Sacrament than just arriving on time for Mass, though it is a good starting point.

Liturgy is a Greek composite word *leitourgia*, which conveyed the description of a public duty, a service to the state undertaken by a citizen. Its elements are *leitos* meaning *public*, and *ergo* meaning *to do*. At the time when Hebrew Scriptures were translated into Greek, they applied *leitourgi'a* to the services performed in the Jerusalem temple. It thus acquired a religious sense as a function of the priests, as they rendered Temple service. Eventually in the Christian tradition, the word acquired theological, devotional, and ecclesiastical significance.

Today, there are two senses in which the word is used. On the one hand, in the western Church, liturgy often means the whole complex of official services, prayers, and sacraments of the Church, as opposed to private devotions. The other sense of the word, relevant to all Eastern Churches, restricts it to the Holy Eucharist.

The *Constitution on the Sacred Liturgy* stated the general goal of Sacred Liturgy: "The Church earnestly desires that all the faithful be led to that full, conscious, and active participation in liturgical celebrations called for by the very nature of the liturgy. Such participation by the Christian people as 'a chosen race, a royal priesthood, a holy nation, God's own people' (1 Peter 2:9; see 2:4-5), is their right and duty by reason of their baptism" (*Constitution on the Sacred Liturgy*, No. 14). Every parish has the responsibility of providing meaningful liturgies for their people, and that is why we build magnificent sanctuaries that evoke a sense of the divine and facilitates the celebration of the Sacraments and prayers.

The *General Instruction of the Roman Missal* (GIRM) notes the importance of "directions about the preparation of people's hearts and minds, and of the places, rites, and texts for the celebration of the Most Holy Eucharist." Since the Eucharist is the "primary and indispensable source from which the faithful are to derive the true Christian Spirit," the entire celebration should be consciously planned and deferentially executed. Although it is hard to find a Scriptural basis for a team that plans and prepares for the celebration of the Eucharist, there is so much to learn from Jesus in setting the stage for celebrating the Passover with his disciples and for His ultimate surrender and sacrifice:

On the first day of Unleavened Bread, when
the Passover lamb was being sacrificed, His
disciples said to Him, "Where do You want
us to go and prepare for You to eat the Passover?" And He sent two of His disciples and
said to them, "Go into the city, and a man
will meet you carrying a pitcher of water;
follow him; and wherever he enters, say to
the owner of the house, 'The Teacher says,'
Where is My guest room in which I may eat
the Passover with My disciples?' And he
himself will show you a large upper room
furnished and ready; prepare for us there."
The disciples went out and came to the city
and found *it* just as He had told them; and
they prepared the Passover (Mk: 14:12-16).

Jesus sent Peter and John to secure a large upper
room and prepare that room for breaking bread
with His disciples. In His plan, he has designed a
place, a cleansing ritual of service and love, and a
meal where he shares His body and blood in
anticipation of His death on the cross. His audience
on that grace-filled evening was his apostles. Jesus
invited them to share in the ritual of foot washing,
even though they did not fully understand it. The
foot washing ritual was a symbol of humble service,
given the extreme disgrace involved in washing
feet in the ancient world, a task usually reserved for
the lowest slave of the house. In fact, Jesus' own

words convey it as such: "If I then, the Lord and the Teacher, washed your feet, you also ought to wash one another's feet. For I gave you an example that you also should do as I did to you" (Jn13:14-15).

Jesus instituted the Holy Eucharist during the Last Supper. He brought the Old Testament tradition of the celebration of the Passover to fulfillment. Passover celebrated the deliverance of the Israelites from the plague of death, where the angel of death passed over (hence Passover) the houses that were sprinkled with the blood of the lamb and ultimately setting them free from bondage in Egypt.

During his last supper, he gave a new meaning and significance to this all-important event in their history. He took two symbols associated with Passover and imbued new meaning as a way to commemorate His own ultimate sacrifice on the cross: "And when He had taken some bread and given thanks, He broke it and gave it to them, saying, "This is My body which is given for you; do this in remembrance of Me." And in the same way He took the cup after they had eaten, saying, "This cup, which is poured out for you, is the new covenant in My blood" (Lk 22: 19 – 20).

These words echoed what he had said earlier in his discourse on the Eucharist in the sixth chapter of the Gospel of John:

"I am the bread of life; he who comes to Me will not hunger, and he who believes in Me will never thirst" (John 6: 35).

Again in verse 51: "I am the living bread that came down out of heaven; if anyone eats of this bread, he will live forever; and the bread also which I will give for the life of the world is My flesh."

And in verses 54-55: "He who eats My flesh and drinks My blood has eternal life, and I will raise him up on the last day. For My flesh is true food, and My blood is true drink."

Thus, Jesus offered himself as the New Lamb of sacrifice at the Passover. He instituted a new priesthood in the order of Melchizedek, through which the apostles were commissioned to commemorate His sacrifice: "Do this in remembrance of me" (Luke 22: 19).

What you have witnessed in the celebration of his last supper is the fact that Jesus has prepared himself fully to share the meal with his apostles, giving new meaning to everything. There is no confusion. Through Words and rituals, signs and symbols, he led them to embrace the New Covenant in his blood. If you think, that was impressive, he was not done yet.

Singing a psalm Jesus entered the garden of Gethsemane. He sang at the prospect of salvation. There is transition here from the upper room to the garden where it all begins.

Liturgical music facilitates and gives meaning to what is being celebrated in the sacrament. The hour has come. Jesus prepared himself in deep prayer for his arrest, His unjust condemnation and trial, His cross-laden journey to Calvary and crucifixion. His prayer was so intense that his sweat turned into blood: "And being in agony He was praying very fervently; and His sweat became like drops of blood, falling upon the ground" (Luke 22: 44). He prayed for the strength to do His father's will. Through prayer, Jesus overcame the fear of death and resolved to surrender his life as a ransom for humanity. "Rise! Let us go! Here comes my betrayer" (Mt: 26:46). After prayer, he calmly met the soldiers.

Every priest and every minister who serves at the altar of the Word and the Eucharist must prepare himself or herself through intense prayer, before entering into the sanctuary to celebrate Jesus' death and resurrection. Beyond logistics, prayerful preparation sets the priest apart, as he stands in the place of Jesus to lead the assembly to Calvary. There is a marvelous sentence in the *Code of Canon Law*. Canon 909 reads: "A priest is not to omit dutifully to prepare himself by prayer before the celebration of the Eucharist, nor afterwards to

omit to make thanksgiving to God." In the words of
Bishop Marc Aillet:

> One can never stress enough the importance
> of the silence preceding the liturgical
> celebration, an inner narthex, where we are
> freed of the concerns, even if legitimate, of
> the secular world, in order to enter the sacred
> space and time where God will reveal his
> Mystery.

Vesting prayers can help transition the priest
from the temporal world to the eternal world of
Jesus. A number of prayers from our tradition
("Prayer before Mass" by St. Thomas Aquinas and
others) are available to everyone in preparation for
Mass. A number of my own parishioners come
early and spend time glancing over the readings.
Praying for the grace of attention to the great
mystery, as well as the gift that only God can give
to awaken one's spiritual senses to see, hear,
recognize, and welcome the Savior into one's life
can only enhance our celebrations.

In the October 2016 issue of *The Wall Street
Journal*, an article William E. Simon titled, "Waking
Up From Spiritual Sleepwalking," introduced his
theses in these words, "Some wag once quipped,
'I'm not asleep, but that doesn't mean I'm awake.'"
This vividly describes many of today's churchgoers.
Though disciplined about attendance, many be-

lievers sleepwalk through faith. In my Catholic tradition, the number of parishioners who regularly attend Mass and truly engage with the church stands between 7 and 18 percent. Sleepwalkers are persons who live their lives in an unconscious state. They are not fully aware of who they are or the larger context of life they are part of—the real purpose in life.

Celestine Chua writes:

> Sleepwalkers look like any of us but are really just physical shells living through their lives as drones Every day they are running around doing various activities such as working, playing, partying, sleeping, but none of it has any relation to life in the bigger picture. This is what they have come to know as life.

Like everything else in life, it is so easy to fall prey to the temptation of sleepwalking through Mass.

After 25 years of ministry in the priesthood, I must admit to finding myself sleepwalking through life and ministry. More and more I find myself just *doing things*. My personal identity is mostly defined by my ministerial functions, rather than the person I must be in Christ. I define myself as a priest because I celebrate Mass regularly for the congregation, not because I have become another Christ, or I have been transformed into His image.

In the series, *Conformed to His Image*, Kenneth D. Boa states, "Any dead fish can float downstream— to swim against the current of our times, we must be spiritually alive." According to Boa, the world defines who we are by what we do, but Sacred Scripture focuses on who we are in Christ and tells us to express that new identity in what we do. In the biblical order of things, what we do should flow out of who we are, not the other way around. If not, our worth and identity will be determined by achievements and accomplishments, and when we stop performing, we cease to be valuable. When people reply to the question, "Who are you?" by what they do, the world responds with another question, "So, what have you done lately?" True participation in the Eucharist is not an act of *doing*; it is first an act of *being*. "Could you not watch one hour with me?" And, "Only one thing is necessary, for Mary has chosen the good part, which shall not be taken away from her" (Luke 10: 42).

In the words of Fr. Alex Rebello, Nazareth is a mystery of humble hiddenness. Jesus spent thirty years in Nazareth wrapped in hiddenness, where no one recognized Him or beheld his glory and splendor as the Word-made-flesh. He was taken for granted, as an ordinary human being. He worked as a carpenter in the suburbs. Thirty years of humble hiddenness and inconspicuousness. Just three short years of public ministry. How over- whelmingly disproportionate! Fr. Rebello asks:

• When there was a whole world waiting to be saved why did Jesus "waste" so much time?

• When time was fast running out why did he spend such a large period of his life apparently doing nothing?

• Do the choices and options of Jesus have something to say to us?

The truth is that Jesus spent 30 years preparing Himself for the day when He would launch His mission and ministry. Contrast that with my own preparation as a priest – 6 years of seminary formation followed by 26 years of priestly service and still continuing. If Nazareth and its humble hiddenness was the fundamental option He made embracing ordinariness and quiet contemplation for 30 years, unraveling the will of His Father and centering on Who He was and is, there is a deeper lesson for his disciples who follow in His footsteps. The same was true about His cousin, John the Baptist, who too spent 30 years preparing for his one-year ministry of announcing the coming of the Messiah. When I compare Jesus' own effectiveness in ministry with my own, it is amply clear to me that there is no comparison. The more we prepare in joyful expectation, the better the results we reap. And that is because the doings flow from one's being. "Success is when preparation meets opportunity."

Quiet contemplation and attentive listening go hand in hand. Like the impoverished couple in Mary Oliver's "The Mockingbirds," we have nothing to offer to the Lord who comes to us in His Word and in His body and blood, except our willingness to be attentive. The truth, according to C.S. Lewis, is that God does not want anything from us. He simply wants us. For the Lord to bless us, we must awaken our spiritual senses. We need to cultivate the gift of undivided attention to the mysteries of God's love.

Kevin Cummins narrated the following story:

A gentleman told me of an experience he had. He said: I was recently driving all night to get to a faraway destination. By morning I still had some distance to travel but was getting very tired. I decided to stop at the next city I came to and park somewhere quiet to catch an hour or two of sleep. Unfortunately, the quiet place I chose happened to be one of the city's major jogging routes. No sooner had I settled back to snooze when there was a knock on my window. Upon looking out I saw a jogger running in place, eager to ask me a question. 'Yes?' 'Excuse me, sir,' the jogger said, 'do you have the time?' I looked at the car clock and answered, '8:15.' The jogger said thank you and left.

I settled back again and was just dozing off when there was another knock on the window...and another jogger. 'Excuse me, sir, do you have the time?' '8:25,' I answered as nicely as I could, but I was getting frustrated. The jogger said thanks and left. Now I could see other joggers passing by and I knew it was only a matter of time before another disturbed my much-needed rest. To avoid the problem, I got out a pen and paper and put a sign in my window that read, 'I do not know the time.' I had just fallen back to sleep when there was another knock on the window. 'Sir, sir? It's 8:45!'"

It is hard for many people to settle down for an hour of prayer. A friend boasted to St. Bernard that he had no distractions. St. Bernard admitted that he had trouble with distractions. One day the two of them were out riding on horseback. St. Bernard said he would give his friend his horse, if he got off his horse and could pray the Our Father without any distractions. His friend got as far as, "Give us this day our daily bread," when he looked at St. Bernard and asked, "Can I have the saddle too?"

The saintly pope who coined the phrase "active participation in the Mass" and used it first was Pope Saint Pius X. He explained it this way: "If you wish to participate in the Mass actively, you must follow with your eye, heart and mouth all that happens on the altar. Further, you must pray with the Priest the holy words said by him in the Name of Christ and which Christ says by him. To associate your heart with the holy feelings, contained in these words, you need to follow all that happens at the altar. When acting in this way you have prayed Holy Mass." Therefore, learning the art of prayer and silence is a prerequisite to active participation in the Mass.

Cardinal Robert Sarah said in his book, *By Living with the Silent God, and in Him, We Ourselves are Silent*: "God's first language is silence. Everything else is a poor translation. In order to understand this language, we must learn to be silent and to rest in God." According to him, silence is not just an idea; rather it is the path that enables human beings to reach God. "Silence is the cloth from which our liturgies ought to be cut out." He continued. "Nothing in them should interrupt the silent atmosphere that is their natural climate." Silence is not the pause between two rituals; rather it is itself fully a ritual. "Mary has chosen the better part," Jesus affirmed, indicating how pleased He was with someone who had set aside everything just to be attentive to every Word that dropped from His lips.

As a priest, many parishioners in the parishes I served, expressed concern about the level of talking and noise in church. Many of them, older folks, are nostalgic about a time when they would walk into a church that was quiet and peaceful before Mass or other liturgical celebrations and provided an ambiance of prayer and a great sense of the Sacred. One would walk gently and prayerfully into the aisles, genuflect or bow, and then enter into the pews only to kneel down for prayer before Mass began. At the conclusion of Mass, parishioners normally knelt for a brief moment of prayer and then would leave quietly, not talking until they were in the vestibule or outside of the Church. How many of us have confessed the sin of 'talking in Church' on a regular basis in days past? Those days are gone.

On my arrival in the United States, I registered myself for doctoral degree in the University of San Francisco. Initially, I was shocked that the graduation ceremony took place in the beautiful campus church. To the credit of the Jesuits, I must say it was conducted in a spirit of prayer and quiet joyfulness. I left that church feeling grateful to God for my personal accomplishment and success. It has bothered many in recent times that churches have moved certain other ceremonies into their church edifices such as school graduations, Christmas concerts and sometimes conferences and talks that often do not deal with religious topics. I am not going to defend one side against another but would like to shed some thoughts that might help one to understand the dynamics of the tension that prevails in our places of worship.

During a retreat, Msgr. Charles Pope narrated a story that I found rather humorous and enlightening:

A young Italian couple went to their parish priest and said that they were poor and could not afford to rent a hall. Might they use the parish courtyard for a brief reception

after the wedding? The Pastor graciously
agreed. But on the day of the wedding heavy
rains made the use of the courtyard
impossible. So, the request was made if
perchance they could use the back of the
church, just for a "brief" reception. They
promised to keep the noise down and only
drink "a little" wine. The pastor reluctantly
agreed. But, as is often the case, the wine
flowed in abundance and the volume
increased. The wine flowed some more, and
the volume went up some more!

The pastor was now fuming in the sacristy
and about to go and throw them out when
his neighboring pastor and friend came by.
He inquired as to the anger of the pastor who
replied, "Listen to all the noise they are
making, and in the house of God, Don
Camillo! And they are drinking much wine!"
"Ah, but Father, they are a poor couple and it
is raining. They had to use your church.
Besides, Jesus went to loud weddings and
made wine in abundance. Surely he
understands!"

The pastor responded, "I know that! You
don't need to quote the bible to me! I know
Jesus went to loud weddings and I know
they drank wine! You don't need to tell me
all that! But then, they did not have the
Blessed Sacrament present!"

That story is definitely powerful and offers many Christological layers of meaning. Contrast this with the Scriptural passage about Jesus whipping the sellers and traders out of the Jerusalem Temple declaring, "My house shall be called a house of prayer" (Matthew 21:13). Msgr. Pope volunteered his viewpoint on this tension: "Keeping the Church with an atmosphere conducive to prayer, while a good value, is not the first and most essential focus of Sunday morning in the Catholic Parish. Rather, it is to provide an atmosphere conducive to the gathering of God's people, so that they may together turn their worship and praise to Him. This will necessarily involve some noise, setting up, some announcements, directions, the singing of hymns and prayers, etc."

It is important to emphasize in the context of the aforementioned dialectic the cultural shifts that have taken place both in our Church and in our wider culture. American society is made up of a diversity of groups and cultures that have helped shape its values. American lifestyle has become very informal in the sense that we rarely dress up. You see students going to class in shorts and T-shirts. Instructors and employees seldom wear a tie, and some may even wear blue jeans or slacks along with comfortable walking shoes. Our children and even adults are on e-gadgets all the time, whether they are traveling or eating or exercising. And our restaurant culture has become anything but formal compared to older days.

After Vatican II, the Church opened its windows to let in some fresh air, as Pope John the XXIII frequently remarked. Priests started celebrating Masses in the vernacular and faced the congregation to include them, because they were a vital component of the service. This is a step in the direction of active participation in the liturgy. As time went by, many other areas of the Church ushered in changes. Nuns gave up their formal habits in favor of informal clothes similar to those worn by the people they served. This paradigm shift in the Church's culture included its attitude towards other faiths, the role of women in the life and prayer of the Church, and so much more. It is fair to say that the modern Church is deeply engaged in the modern world. Archbishop Gregory Aymond described this phenomenon best: "The Church, by its teaching and discipleship, has something to say to the world. At the same time, the world is saying something to the Church."

If a pastor is going to enforce strict silence before, during and after the liturgical celebrations, he will ride roughshod over the feelings, sentiments and even cultural expectations of a new world order, as well as a new Church order. Whether we agree with it or not, there is so much emphasis in our parishes today on becoming places where people are welcomed in an ambiance of inclusion and outreach—characteristic marks of the historical

Jesus. I have met many newcomers in my parish who have fled from the harsh rebuke and excessive discipline of certain communities of faith. I have also encountered many who have fled the Church altogether. I asked someone why he was at a particular parish, driving more than an hour every Sunday, he responded without hesitation, "There is so much joy in this Church." The house of God, where God and His people meet, is and should be a place of joy. Unfortunately, there are many in our communities for whom the word joy is not the best description of their faith. They consider themselves faithful people, who are often there because of a sense of obligation or fear or deep responsibility, rather than joy.

Like the older sibling in the parable of the Prodigal Son, refusing to go into the house of joy and celebration, because his younger brother had come home from a life of dissipation and depravity, some prefer to stay outside the house of joy. The father went outside the house of joy, outside the house of party to invite the older brother in with the words: "Son, you have always been with me, and all that is mine is yours. But we had to celebrate and rejoice, for this brother of yours was dead and has begun to live and was lost and has been found" (Luke 15: 31-32).

Where God is, there is joy in the house. Our Churches are places of joyful celebration, because of His mercy and thoughtfulness. That is why the Psalmist exclaimed, " I was glad when they said to me, 'Let us go to the house of the LORD'" (Psalm 122: 1).

In defense of pastors who struggle to find ways to keep an ambiance of prayer and quiet joyfulness in our churches, Church leadership needs to balance welcome, hospitality and the creation of the sense of community, with the fact that it is also a place of prayer and worship before, during, and after Mass. I would recommend educating our communities about the need for quiet and solitude as parishioners enter into God's house of prayer, without offending or irritating anyone and without losing the spirit of joyful celebration.

St. Josemaría wrote that "silence is the door-keeper of the interior life." He encouraged the faithful living in the middle of the world to seek moments of more intense recollection, compatible with hard work. He underscored the importance of preparing well for the Eucharistic celebration. In an environment permeated by new technologies, Christians need to find time and space to draw close to God, where their senses and imagination, their mind and will are as recollected as possible.

Pope Francis, while addressing issues related to the media and Internet in the life of a Christian, said that people need to recover certain sense of deliberateness and calm. Can you find an oasis of quiet and joy in the midst of chaos? In her book, *Leadership and the New Science*, Margaret J. Wheatley wrote: "Whatever your personal beliefs and experiences, I invite you to consider that we need a new worldview to navigate this chaotic time. We cannot hope to make sense using our old maps. It won't help to dust them off or reprint them in bold colors. The more we rely on them, the more disoriented we become. They cause us to focus on the wrong things and blind us to what's significant. Using them, we will journey only to greater chaos." According to her, listening is a simple act that requires of us to be present, and that takes practice. We have to be willing to sit there and listen. She said, "Change always involves a dark night when everything falls apart. Yet if this period of dissolution is used to create new meaning, then chaos ends, and new order emerges."

The things we fear most in our places of worship—fluctuations, commotions, noise, and restlessness—should become the primary sources of creativity in our spiritual quest and practice. There is no substitute to confronting the challenges that we face and channeling them to spiritual energies that would facilitate our worship and prayer in the modern chaotic world.

I read the following account of two men who went to the same church but came away feeling differently about their spiritual experience.

A certain man went to Church one Sunday. He frowned when the organist missed a note during the opening hymn. He stared menacingly at two adolescents talking to each other, when the congregation was at prayer. During the Scripture readings, he kept looking impatiently at his watch. During the sermon, he felt mighty pleased with himself, when he caught the preacher making a slip of the tongue. When the collection basket was passed, he felt that the usher was watching to see how much he gave. He was tight-lipped during all of the hymn singing. As he slipped out a side door during the closing hymn, he muttered to himself, "That was terrible. What a bunch of clods. Never again!"

A certain other man went to Church one Sunday and was edified by the organist's moving rendition of "Amazing Grace." He marveled at the sight of a father exchanging hugs with the little child draped over his shoulder. He had but one thought when the collection basket was passed: "Some of what I give will be used to serve the needy. Am I giving enough?" He listened attentively to the Scripture readings, which spoke of God's incredible love for the human family. He heard something in the sermon that helped him with a question that had bothered him for a long time. He enthusiastically joined in the singing of the closing hymn of praise. As he left the Church, he said to himself, "How good it is to be here and share in the experience of the Presence of God!"

Both men had gone to the same church, on the same Sunday, and each had found exactly what he was looking for.

The question we all need to ask ourselves is, what are we looking for in the Eucharistic experience? Attitude is everything. Choosing the proper attitude! Viktor Frankl said, "There is a freedom that no one can ever take from you—your choice of how you are going to respond to the circumstances given to you." My hope and prayer is that all of us will enter God's house with the ardent desire to meet Jesus in the breaking of the Word and the breaking of the Bread, as well as in all our brothers and sisters gathered together in worship.

In the Sacrament of the Eucharist, some of us tend to miss the big picture, because we choose instead to get caught up in the trivialities. By making minor changes and adjustments in your thinking and altering your responses to situations, you can elevate yourself from the melancholy that comes when you focus on the trivialities. Turn your mind, emotions, and thoughts from the situations before you, even when they seem hard to rise above and look at the bigger picture. Why are you here in the Assembly of God? What are you looking for from God's gift of Himself in the Eucharist?

Liturgical Vestments

"Nothing can be too beautiful for God"
Pope Benedict XVI.

Liturgical vestments worn by priests during sacramental celebrations have evolved over time. The Church adapted them from the Graeco-Roman world and their religious culture. According to Chris Labarde, "As the secular fashions changed, the clothing used for Mass and other liturgies began to lose their secular connection and become primarily liturgical. As the vestments have continued to develop over the past 1,300 years or so, they have become markedly different from our secular clothing and so the symbol they provide, of Liturgy being set apart from everyday life has become more pronounced." The Office for the Liturgical Celebrations of the Supreme Pontiff states:

Beyond the historical circumstances, the sacred vestments had an important function in the liturgical celebrations: In the first place, the fact that they are not worn in ordinary life, and thus possess a "liturgical" character, helps one to be detached from the everyday and its concerns in the celebration

of divine worship. Furthermore, the ample
form of the vestments, the alb, for example,
the dalmatic and the chasuble, put the
individuality of the one who wears them in
second place, in order to emphasize his
liturgical role. One might say that the
"camouflaging" of the minister's body by the
vestments depersonalizes him in a way; it is
that healthy depersonalization that de-
centers the celebrating minister and recognizes the true protagonist of the liturgical
action: Christ. The form of the vestments,
therefore, says that the liturgy is celebrated
"in persona Christi" and not in the priest's
own name. He who performs a liturgical
function does not do so as a private person,
but as a minister of the Church and an
instrument in the hands of Jesus Christ. The
sacred character of the vestments also has to
do with their being donned according to
what is prescribed in the Roman Ritual.

According to the *General Instructions of the
Roman Missal* (#335), vestments used in the Mass
have twofold purpose: "These should therefore
symbolize the function of each ministry. But at the
same time the vestments should also contribute to
the beauty of the rite." Today, a priest wears an alb,
cincture, stole and chasuble. There are prayers that
accompany the vesting of each of these items, (we
will call them Vesting Prayers) shedding light on

their meaning and significance for both the celebrant and the liturgy. Prayers help the priest move from the mundane and ordinary gesture of vesting to what is deeply spiritual and profound, leading the him into the realm of the transcendent, since he will now don the mantle of Christ and act *in persona Christi*. Let us look at the individual vestments and their prayers.

Alb

The alb is a long white garment, which flows from shoulders to ankles and has sleeves extending to the wrists. Adapted from the Graeco-Roman world, the alb is similar to the soutane worn in the Middle East. Some modern style albs have collars, which preclude wearing an amice. The alb reminds the priest of the new and immaculate clothing that every Christian has received through baptism. The alb is, therefore, a symbol of the sanctifying grace received in the first sacrament and is also con-sidered to be a symbol of the purity of heart that is necessary to enter into the joy of the eternal vision of God in heaven. The prayer the priest says as he dons the alb expresses this powerful sentiment: "Make me white, O Lord, and cleanse my heart; that being made white in the Blood of the Lamb I may deserve an eternal reward."

Cincture

The priest secures the alb around the waist with a cincture, a long and thick cord with tassels at the ends. It may be white or the same liturgical color as the other vestments of the day. In the Graeco-Roman world, the cincture was like a belt. Spiritually, the cincture reminds the priest of the admonition of St. Peter: "Gird the loins of your understanding; live soberly; set all your hope on the gift to be conferred on you when Jesus Christ appears. As obedient sons, do not yield to the desires that once shaped you in your ignorance. Rather, become holy yourselves in every aspect of your conduct, after the likeness of the Holy One who called you" (I Peter 1:13-15). The vesting prayer is "Gird me, O Lord, with the cincture of purity, and quench in my heart the fire of concupiscence, that the virtues of continence and chastity may abide in me."

Stole

The stole is the distinct element of the clothing of the ordained minister. It is always worn in the celebration of the sacraments and sacramentals. The stole is a long cloth, about four inches wide and of the same color as the chasuble. The priest wears it around the neck like a scarf. It is secured at the waist with the cincture. The stole, too, is of ancient origin. Rabbis wore prayer shawls with tassels as a sign of their authority. The stole thus reminds the priest of the 'state of his ordained office' and dignity, as well as his duty to preach the Word the God with courage. The minister dons the stole with the prayer: " Lord, restore the stole of immortality, which I lost through the collusion of our first parents, and, unworthy as I am to approach Thy sacred mysteries, may I yet gain eternal joy."

Finally, he puts on the chasuble, "the vestment proper to him who celebrates the Holy Mass" (The Office for the liturgical Celebrations of the Supreme Pontiff). Over the centuries, various styles of chasubles have emerged. Derived from the Latin word *casula* meaning "house," the chasuble in the Graeco-Roman world was like a cape that completely covered the body and protected the person from inclement weather. The prayer for the donning of the chasuble references the exhortation of St. Paul in the Letter to the Colossians 3:14: "Above all these things [put on] charity, which is the bond of perfection." The formal vesting prayer is: "O Lord, who has said, 'My yoke is sweet and My burden light," grant that I may so carry it as to merit Thy grace'" (Matthew 11:30).

Liturgical vestments are an integral part of the celebration of the Sacraments, as they set the tone and create an ambiance of prayer and solemnity. It sets the priest on a trajectory of transcendence, whereby the priest is transported to God's eternal presence, standing or acting *in persona Christi*. The chasuble worn over all other vestments now fulfills, at least symbolically, the exhortation of St. Paul, "by being of the same mind, having the same love, being in full accord and of one mind" (Phil. 2:2). The ordained minister approaches the altar with the heart and mind of Jesus. As he stands before the people of God, there is only one attitude that defines his ministry. It is love. Like the Master who removed his outer garments and wrapped himself with a towel, the garment of service at the Last Supper, the priest too takes off the mantle of privilege and transforms it into the apron of service (John Shea). Rather than evoking sentiments of power, authority and privilege, the ordained minister should exhibit deeply spiritual qualities of humility, hospitality, and service.

Liturgical Colors

Did you know your surroundings might be influencing your emotions and state of mind? Do you notice that certain places bother you? Or that certain places are especially relaxing and calming? As the Church moves through the year, it provides many symbols to remind us of the significance of seasons and days. Color can be highly expressive and reflective of mood and meaning. Colored vestments and hangings have been among the most prominent symbols used in the Catholic Church. The colors adorn the Sacred Space and call attention to the nature of the season or the feasts being celebrated. The most commonly used vestment colors, as well as Church decorations, are white, red, green, and purple.

The Church used only white until the 4th Century. The other colors followed soon afterwards. In the words of the *Catholic Encyclopedia*:

The variety of liturgical colors in the Church arose from the mystical meaning attached to them. Thus white, the symbol of light, typifies innocence and purity, joy and glory; red, the language of fire and blood, indicates burning charity and the martyrs' generous sacrifice; green, the hue of plants and trees, bespeaks the hope of life eternal; violet, the gloomy cast of the mortified, denotes affliction and melancholy; while black, the universal emblem of mourning, signifies the sorrow of death and the somberness of the tomb.

White, as a festive color symbolic of joy and victory, is the color proper to feasts of the Lord, including the seasons of Easter and Christmas, but not for His Passion. It is also the liturgical color for feasts of Mary, All Saints, Chair of Peter, Conversion of Paul, the Nativity of John the Baptist, St. John the Evangelist, the angels, and for saints who are not martyrs. White reminds us of the resurrection and therefore is appropriate at funerals. Gold is reserved for solemn occasions.

Red (the color of blood) is proper to days when we celebrate the sufferings of Jesus, like Passion (Palm) Sunday and Good Friday. Feasts of the apostles and evangelists and celebrations of martyrs also call for red. Red (the color of fire) recalls the Holy Spirit and is proper for Pentecost and for the sacrament of Confirmation.

Purple (or violet) reminds us of the violet flower that bows its head and is a symbol of humility, repentance, and penance. Vestments of purple or violet appear during the seasons of Advent and Lent. Lent is a season of prayer, fasting and almsgiving—a quiet season of reflection. Purple or violet dye cost a great deal in the 1st Century. An early Christian, Lydia from Thyatira, made her living from the purple dye trade and used her profits to support St Paul in his missionary work (Acts 16: 14-15).

Green, the color of life, renewal, nature, and energy, associates with growth, harmony, freshness, safety, fertility, and the environment. It also stands for lack of experience and the need for growth. Green is on display everywhere in plants and trees. During Ordinary Time, it symbolizes life, anticipation, and hope.

Rose pink is an optional color for the Third Sunday of Advent and Fourth Sunday of Lent. On both days, the Entrance Antiphon calls us to rejoice, so pink vestments mark a softening of the penitential tone of the season. It expresses joy and conveys the concept of rejoicing, for redemption is so close at hand.

Is there a dress code for Mass attendance?

Neither Scripture nor the teachings of the Church and its canons say much about a proper dress code for those attending sacred worship. 1 Timothy 2:9 addressed this issue more from a perspective of "good deeds" or "holy hands" which reinforces the truth that one must come from a place of goodness, compassion and love rather than merely dressing up. "Therefore I want the men in every place to pray, lifting up holy hands, without wrath and dissension. Likewise, *I want* women to adorn themselves with proper clothing, modestly and discreetly, not with braided hair and gold or pearls or costly garments, but rather by means of good works, as is proper for women making a claim to godliness" (1 Timothy 2: 8-11).

Historically, a lot of attention was given to cleanliness and solemnity on Sunday. Dressing up for worship resulted, not from a theological or Scriptural teaching, but from the influence of culture on worshiping communities. According to Carl Raschke, religious studies professor at the University of Denver, the early church was anti-hierarchical and adopted a "come as you are" approach to worship, welcoming outcasts and the disenfranchised, who could not dress in fine clothes.

Medieval Christians, being common folk, could not dress up for Church. Only the wealthy could afford to buy expensive clothing. Later, industrialization and urbanization gave rise to a new middle class, who could afford fine linen. They began dressing up for social events, including worship. In this regard, we cannot ignore the influence of the Victorian Era on the Church. When we speak about a dress code for Church worship, the casualness of

Sunday attire among parishioners today upsets many who demand their pastors and congregations to take note, stating that it is about respect and reverence for God.

As I referred to earlier, here in America, we are casual when it comes to how we dress for just about everything today. And that has definitely exhibited itself in our places of worship. First, I want you to know that the Church is really happy to see you at Mass. No one should ever judge you on what you wear or do not. There is only one judge. In my opinion, He does not care about makeup, however little or too much. He doesn't care about frizzy hair or holes in tights or tattoos or body piercings. In 1 Samuel 16:17, the Lord said to Samuel, "Do not look at his appearance or at the height of his stature, because I have rejected him; for God *sees* not as man sees, for man looks at the outward appearance, but the Lord looks at the heart." There are lots of things about us that we can do better but worrying too much about what we wear or what others wear should not be at the top of our priorities. Having said that, I do want to offer some suggestions.

Years ago, I heard a story dating back to the time of miniskirts. A little girl accompanied her mother, who wore a miniskirt, to a carnival. In the huge crowd, the girl got separated from her mother and stood in a corner crying. When a volunteer noticed the little girl, he approached her and asked what the matter was. She said, "I can't find my mother." "Okay," said the good man. "Tell me her name." She said, "Mom." That did not help. So, he further questioned her about her mom's dress. "What is your mom wearing?" "A skirt," she answered. "Why didn't you hold on tight to your mother's skirt, so you wouldn't get separated?" he asked. Without hesitation, she said, "I couldn't reach it." This is a funny story, but what I want to underscore is the fact that modesty should be the norm both for women and men, when it comes to our manner of dress in a place of worship and prayer.

The Catechism of the Catholic Church (Nos. 2521-2524) offers several paragraphs on the topic of modesty, saying in part: "Modesty is decency. It inspires one's choice of clothing. . . . Modesty inspires a way of life that makes it possible to resist the allurements of fashion and the pressures of prevailing ideologies." We should not dress in a way that would attract undue attention of others and become a source of distraction for our fellow worshippers.

St. James, in his epistle (2: 2-4), warned against the sin of partiality and discrimination among worshippers based on how the faithful look or dress:

If a man comes into your assembly with a gold ring and dressed in fine clothes, and there also comes in a poor man in dirty clothes, and you pay special attention to the one who is wearing the fine clothes, and say, 'You sit here in a good place,' and you say to the poor man, 'You stand over there, or sit down by my footstool,' have you not made distinctions among yourselves, and become judges with evil motives?"

One of the priests living with me narrated this experience he had in a parish where he served as pastor. Two weeks before his assigned date at the new Church, he arrived incognito looking dirty, unshaven, smelly, and homeless. He walked into the Church unattended by anyone stationed at the front doors to greet and meet people. He sat on a pew at the rear, only to be frowned upon by some people around him. Some declined even to exchange the sign of peace with him. The newly appointed pastor wanted to learn about his new parishioners and their sense of compassion and hospitality, especially towards the lowliest members of the congregation. While it is important to dress moderately well for worship, or for that matter to any respectable event, we have a duty and obligation to welcome everyone who walks into the House of God and reach out in compassionate and loving ways. We are a community of caring and service. In the words of Raschke:

Adopting a dress code would not only be suicidal for American Christians who are swimming against the stream of casual secularism, it would be antithetical to what Christianity sees increasingly as its abiding mission—to reach those who are marginalized and 'don't fit in.'

One of the more popular shows on Black Entertainment Television (BET) is the gospel music talent show, *Sunday Best*. Gospel music legend Kirk Franklin hosts the show and offers the gospel equivalent and alternative to popular talent shows like *American Idol* and *The Voice*. "The show, *Sunday Best*, may be a recent phenomenon," says Tony Carter, Pastor of East Point Church, but the idea is not new." He goes on to list five Sunday Bests offered at a traditional Black Church:

1. Sunday Best Dress: I don't think we should make a huge deal out of one's dress, so long as it is modest (cf. 1 Tim. 2:9). When I see the seasoned saints coming into the sanctuary dressed intentionally in some of their finest attire, I am reminded of the gravity of worship and the intentional thought that should go into worship each Sunday, as we offer to God our best.
2. Sunday Best Fellowship: Sunday was for fellowship. And fellowship was always best on Sunday.
3. Sunday Best Welcome: In the traditional black church, there are no strangers. I have belonged to and served in black churches in several states. I

have visited many more. I can honestly say that I have rarely ever felt a stranger.

4. Sunday Best Forgiveness: The black church is not just the place of second chances, or third chances, but she has seemingly taken our Lord's admonition to heart and has been willing to forgive her fallen leaders "seventy times seven" (Mt. 18: 21-22).

5. Sunday Best Music: When people think of the traditional black church, they generally think of two things: preaching and singing. And of the two, the latter is probably the most notable. The black church has long been the bastion of great singers and performers.

I am always learning from other parishes and sometimes from other Christian Churches. I have tried to track the origins of the expression, "Sunday Best," without much success. But it gives me great pleasure to know that it means much more than a dress code for some of our Churches. It embraces the whole spirit of the liturgy and has so much to do with hospitality, inclusion, and more.

Clothing is one of the ways we communicate with others, and what we wear is never a purely personal matter. Think about some of the messages we send by the way we dress:

At a party for instance, "I would like people to notice me."

In a business meeting, we like to communicate, "I am very confident."

Or, it could mean any of the following contingent on the circumstances:

"I want to look seductive."
"I want to hide."
"I want to be respectful and reverent."
"I want to be comfortable."

The way you dress can also affect your mood or shape the way you feel. When a soldier dons his uniform, he will feel different than he does when in street clothes. In some situations, the way we dress can make or break us. Worshiping together as a community transforms us into the Mystical Body of Christ. Worship is definitely an experience of the heart. Scripture has always underscored its principle that, for God, worship is all about what is internal, not external. There is a point to be made for dressing up for Church.

I invite you to consider what it would mean for you to dress for worship. Would you feel good and reverent sitting in the pews before God? Would it make a difference for you and for the people around you, and if so what would you wear? What we wear to public worship does matter in more ways than we think. I would not demand a certain dress code to the detriment of our younger generation, in particular, who might empty the pews. Like everything else, spiritual maturity and growth eventually prompt corrective measures in the faithful. In recent years, I have witnessed an interesting phenomenon—more and more people dressing themselves in the liturgical colors of the day. Liturgical colors orient us to the season of the Church's liturgical year and help to engage the sense of sight in worship. This is something I encourage, since it evokes a sense of expectation and joy especially during festive occasions.

Introductory Rites

1. The Entrance Procession.

Once the people have gathered, the priest and ministers, clad in the sacred vestments, go in procession to the altar. . . . During the procession to the altar, the Entrance chant takes place (*General Instruction of the Roman Missal*).

During our school Masses, one of the children climbs up to the Ambo and announces something like this: "Welcome to _____ Church. Please stand as we sing our entrance hymn and welcome Fr. _____ our celebrant."

There are multiple viewpoints as to whether the procession is to welcome the priest, set the sacrament in motion, or something else. The entrance procession marks the beginning of the Eucharistic celebration. From a theological per-spective, entrance processions remind us of our sojourn in this world, that we are indeed pilgrims. Liturgical notes in the *New Liturgy of the Revised Roman Missal* remind us, "The entrance procession symbolized that journey from the world outside the doors at the back of the church, to our heavenly destination, symbolized by the sanctuary at the front of the church. In that journey, Christ is not only our goal, symbolized by the altar, but He also accompanies us on the way in the person of the priest."

The priest and anyone who walks with him in the procession represent the congregation. Like disciples on the road to Emmaus, the entire Church is indeed on the road accompanied by the Stranger moving towards the New Emmaus, where Jesus will open the Scriptures and break bread for us. The procession begins from the outside—from our homes, our places of work, from everything that defines who we are and what we do.

Between the time you leave home and find a space for yourself and your family in the pew, a lot can happen. Your kids are arguing and fighting in the car. Someone cuts in front of you, sending you into a nervous whimper or worse. The roads may be wet or filled with snow or, all of a sudden, traffic becomes overcrowded. When you arrive at the parking lot, you keep circling around looking for a parking space and there isn't one. As you arrive at the Church, there is no one to greet you and help you find a seat. Life is an unexpected turn of surprises at every turn.

Now, it is the time to compose yourself and get into the spirit of the Mass. Thus, it becomes an imperative to leave home early and arrive in time, time, so you are ready for the procession, a symbol of the Emmaus journey, and to welcome the stranger, who is Jesus. You don't celebrate Mass alone, trying to focus and decipher on your own. You open your heart and Jesus speaks to you and opens the Scriptures to you during the Sacrament. Jesus enters into a deep and profound conversation about your unanswered questions and unresolved challenges, as you listen to him in the breaking of the Word. It becomes paramount that you arrive in time to be fully on the road with your fellow disciples, as they process into the sanctuary—the New Emmaus.

2. The Greeting

Customs and rituals involved in greeting someone differ from culture to culture. In the United States, greetings are casual when they meet one another—a handshake, a smile, a "hello." In France, people shake hands with their friends and often kiss them on both cheeks, upon meeting and leaving. I was recently in Japan, where the common greeting for men and women is to bow. While traveling by the Shinkansen, the high-speed train, every time the railway crew walked into the coach, they would bow respectfully at the entrance and then inspect or offer service to their customers. Russians offer a firm handshake, while maintaining direct eye contact. *Namaste* or *namaskar* is the Indian way of greeting one another. Wherever they are on the street, in the house, in public transport or on the phone, when Hindus meet people they know or strangers with whom they want to initiate a conversation, *"Namaste"* is the customary courtesy greeting with which to begin a conversation and is often the salutation with which to end an encounter. Literally, it means, "I bow to you." The Bhutanese ask, "Is your body well?" while the Taiwanese ask, "Have you eaten?" as they meet and greet one another. Before visiting a foreign country, it is recommended to check on the various meaning of hand gestures. A visitor may inadvertently find himself or herself in an awkward situation. So, it is no surprise that Mass begins with a greeting. After all, Mass is an encounter on many levels. It is a Sacred Liturgy and the greeting at the beginning of Mass is formal and ritualized.

The priest greets the congregation with the following words, "The grace of the Lord Jesus Christ, and the love of God, and the communion of the Holy Spirit, be with you all." These words taken from the second letter of Paul to the Corinthians (13:14) underscore the deep relationship between Jesus and us as we gather in prayer. It means that here, at this celebration, we have in our midst the Lord Jesus, just as he was walking with the disciples on the road to Emmaus, or near to those who saw Him and heard Him in the towns and villages of Galilee, or by the lakeside, or on the mount. In this greeting, Paul draws on the three attributes of God—grace, love and communion. These three divine attributes are now imparted to us. Grace and love define who God is and how he relates with us. The word communion reminds us of the presence of the Holy Spirit in us that make us sons and daughters of a common Father, and brothers and sisters of Jesus Christ. At the Eucharistic celebration, we gather together, not as individuals with our own personal concerns and preoccupations, but as a community marked by the presence, grace and love of Jesus Christ, who pledged to abide in us "where two or three are gathered together."

From Christianity's inception, it existed as a community. No one could be a Christian in isolation, but only together in communion or fellowship of love, after all we are made in the image and likeness of a God, who is a community of three persons. Christianity means a common life, "See how they love one another." It happens so often in our church communities that people struggle with the concept of communion. Someone once sent me an email stating that she did not want to hold or shake hands with anyone during Mass. Her comments were made in the context of praying the "Our Father," during which the congregation reached out to one another and held hands. She also said that the only person she wanted to hold hands or shake hands with was the priest and no one else. Church is a family where the members love and care for one another, carrying each other's burden. Individualism or self-centeredness has no place in God's Church, but they are in fact attributes of a world outside of

Jesus. One of the characteristic features of the post-resurrection stories is that Jesus always appeared to his disciples in groups, never individually, when he broke bread with them or cooked fish on the shore of the lake. Even when he personally invited Thomas to put his hands on His side, it was in the presence of the other disciples. His unbelief was their unbelief; Peter's denial was the community's denial. We humans in our inter-connectedness share each other's burdens and weaknesses and feel the need to commune with God as a people. Nowhere else, is this manifested more powerfully than in the celebration of the Eucharist.

The congregation responds, "And with your Spirit," acknowledging the grace, presence, and Spirit of Christ in the spirit of the priest who presides at Mass. This understanding of the dialogue was not uncommon among the Fathers of Church. For example, St. John Chrysostom wrote in a Pentecost homily:

If the Holy Spirit were not in our Bishop [referring to Bishop Flavian of Antioch] when he gave the peace to all shortly before ascending to his holy sanctuary, you would not have replied to him all together, And with your spirit. This is why you reply with this expression . . . reminding yourselves by this reply that he who is here does nothing of his own power, nor are the offered gifts the work of human nature, but it is the grace of the Spirit present and hovering over all things which prepared that mystic sacrifice.

The Sacrament of Holy Orders configures the priest or bishop who celebrates Mass to Christ. The Spirit of Christ is in him in a unique way that is unlike any other non-ordained member of the congregation. The priest acts *in persona Christi*. That is, Christ personally ministers through him in such a way that we say that Christ is the true priest and celebrant of every Mass. The phrase, "and with your spirit," is an acknowledgment and statement of faith in this fact. The congregation says in effect, "We acknowledge the Spirit, presence, and grace of Christ in your spirit father."

This understanding of the Greeting and response is confirmed by the fact that only a Bishop, priest, or deacon may give the greeting, "The Lord be with you," and hence receive the response, "and with your spirit." For example, the *General Instruction for the Celebration of Mass in the Absence of a Priest* says: "The layperson is not to use words that are proper to a priest or deacon and is to omit rites that are too readily associated with the Mass, for example, greetings—especially, "The Lord be with you"—and dismissals, since these might give the impression that the layperson is a sacred minister" (SCAP #39).

3. Penitential Rite

The presider greets the people of God and invites them to seek God's mercy and forgiveness. Although this rite does not replace the Sacrament of Penance, it serves to remind us of the reconciliation Christ has won for us. We, as a community formed of saints and sinners, stand in need of God's mercy. The priest invites us to acknowledge our sinfulness. The penitential Rite that includes confession, penance, and absolution is deeply rooted in Sacred Scripture and tradition. 1 John 1: 9 states, "If we confess our sins, He is faithful and righteous to forgive us our sins and to cleanse us from all unrighteousness." St. James, in his letter, exhorts his readers to confess their sins to one another: "Therefore, confess your sins to one another, and pray for one another, that you may be healed" (5:16). These two verses taken together form the foundation for the Confiteor. Confessing sins at the beginning of mass was indeed a tradition in the early church. In an early treatise, the Didache (Teaching) states, "But every Lord's day, gather yourselves together and break bread, and give thanksgiving after having confessed your transgressions, that your sacrifice may be pure." According to Patrick Pierce:

There is evidence, though, that it may have been a part of the ceremony before Christianity itself. In the ancient Jewish sin offerings, the priest began by laying his hands on the hands on the animal and saying: "Ah, Jehovah! I have committed iniquity; I have transgressed; I have sinned—I and my house. Oh, then, Jehovah, I entreat Thee, cover over the iniquities, the transgressions, and the sins which I have committed" (quoted in *The Temple—Its Ministry and Services* by Alfred Edersheim, page 101).

Pierce further quotes St. Augustine, who in the 5th Century noted that " [n]o sooner have you heard the word *Confiteor* than you strike your breast. What does this mean except that you wish to bring to light what is concealed in the breast, and by this act to cleanse your hidden sins?" (*Sermo de Verbis Domini*, 13).

The basic words of the Confiteor began appearing in written records of the Mass itself around the 11th Century. See *New Advent History of the Confiteor*. They became a part of the accepted Order of Mass at the Council of Trent, when the Church had to institutionalize the Order of Mass from the threat of increasing Protestant changes to the liturgy."

There is so much beauty and meaning in the Confiteor. It lays out the attitude of participants as they enter into the house of God. They acknowledge their sinfulness, while beating their breasts in deep sorrow. It mirrors the publican, who walked into the temple of God with a humble and repentant Spirit, and "standing far off, would not even lift his eyes to heaven, but beat his breast." His prayer was brief: "God be merciful to me a sinner." He has nothing to offer to God to compensate for his sin. We come to the Eucharistic celebration empty, impoverished, despised, bankrupt and despicable, and deeply wanting human beings. We have nothing to bank on except the mercy of God. Through the Confiteor, we put ourselves in the shoes and mindset of a man who, in the words of Jesus, went away justified because he had humbled himself before God, confessing he was a sinner. He was there because he needed God's redeeming mercy.

There is a story that expresses this truth about God mercy powerfully.

A man dies and goes to heaven. St. Peter meets him at the Pearly Gates and says, "Here's how it works. You need 100 points to make it into heaven. You tell me all the good things you've done, and I give you a certain number of points for each item, depending on how good it was. When you reach 100 points, you get in."

"Okay," the man says, "I was married to the same woman for 50 years and never cheated on her and loved her deep in my heart."

"That's wonderful," says St. Peter, "that's worth two points!"

"Only two points?" the man says.

"Well, I attended church all my life and supported its ministry with my tithes and service."

"Terrific!" says St. Peter. "That's certainly worth a point."

"One point!?!! I started a soup kitchen in my city and also worked in a shelter for homeless veterans."

"Fantastic, that's good for two more points," St. Peter says.

"Two points!?!!" Exasperated, the man cries, "At this rate, the only way I'll get into heaven is by the grace of God."

"Bingo! 100 points! Come on in!"

"For by grace you have been saved through faith, and that not of yourselves; it is the gift of God, not of works, lest anyone should boast" (Ephesians 2: 8-9).

4. Gloria

We sing the Gloria or "Glory to God in the highest" in Church on Sundays and other solemn feasts, except during Lent and Advent. According to Msgr. Charles Pope, the Gloria was not created originally for Mass. "It is and heirloom from the treasure of ancient church hymns. Indeed, it is a precious remnant of a literature now mostly lost but once certainly very rich. These hymns imitated and borrowed from biblical themes."

It started as a simple hymn, but the Council of Remini in 359 declared it as doctrine and integrated the hymn into the Mass. In the 6th Century, Pope Symmachus permitted its use on Sundays and feasts of martyrs, but only at a Mass presided over by a Bishop. Pope Gregory allowed its use at the Easter Mass, even if the Celebrant was a priest. It was not until the 11th Century that the Church dropped the distinction of allowing it only for Bishops' Masses. This was due to continual requests that it be allowed. Today, the Gloria is said at all masses of a festive character outside of penitential seasons.

One of the retired priests that I minister with at our parish always prefaces the singing of the Gloria with the words, "Are you grateful in your heart for something that occurred during this week. Is there anything for which you want to praise the Lord?" Glory to God in the highest! This context and condition are necessary, if the angelic promise of peace on earth is to become a reality. "To 'give glory to God in the highest' means to acknowledge Him and worship Him and love Him above all else, and to live of His Word" (Walter E. Orthwein). Like the shepherds, we hear and celebrate the announcement of the good news of Jesus' birth— that God has visited his people, that God is Emmanuel (God with us). "Let us now go to Bethlehem and see this thing that has come to pass, which the Lord has made know to us." Like those shepherds, we must embark on our journey to encounter Jesus, the Savior. In singing this hymn, we assume the simplicity and mindset of the shepherds, who eagerly and confidently surrounded the Word Made Flesh in adoration and praise.

5. The Collect—Prayer before the Readings

The introductory Rite concludes with a prayer, which in the Latin Church is termed "The Collect Prayer." The presider summons the community into prayer saying, "Let us pray." He allows for a period of silence, then sums up or collects (hence the name collect) or gathers the prayers of the community with the Collect Prayer. The community ratifies the prayer led by the Presider with a corporate, "Amen."

To understand the structure and significance of the Collect Prayer, let us look at the prayer used for the Third Sunday of Ordinary Time.

God of salvation, the splendor of your glory dispels the darkness of the earth, for in Christ we behold the nearness of your kingdom. Now, make us quick to follow where he beckons, eager to embrace the tasks of the gospel. We ask this through our Lord Jesus Christ, your Son, who lives and reigns with you in the unity of the Holy Spirit, God forever and ever. R. Amen.

The Collect Prayer consists of five segments:
1. It is addressed to God—*God of salvation*
2. It speaks about some attribute of God or to one of his saving acts—*The splendor of your glory dispels*

the darkness of the earth.

3. The petition—*Now, make us quick to follow where he beckons, eager to embrace the tasks of the gospel.*

4. The reason for which we ask—*For in Christ we behold the nearness of your kingdom.*

5. The conclusion—*We ask this through our Lord Jesus Christ, your Son, who lives and reigns with you in the unity of the Holy Spirit, God forever and ever.*

How much Mass can I miss and still not miss Mass?

The *General Instruction of the Roman Missal* states clearly the purpose of the introductory Rite:

> The rites that precede the Liturgy of the Word, namely, the Entrance, the Greeting, the Penitential Act, the Kyrie, the *Gloria in excelsis* (Glory to God in the highest) and Collect, have the character of a beginning, an introduction, and a preparation. Their purpose is to ensure that the faithful, who come together as one, establish communion and dispose themselves properly to listen to the Word of God and to celebrate the Eucharist worthily (Article 46).

I would like to underscore the words "establish communion" used by GIRM. It is important that we as a Church gather well in advance so that this communion can take place. The GIRM further develops this theme, stating that the Gathering Hymn fosters union and creates an ambiance in which one can experience the mystery in all its beauty and fullness:

> Its purpose is to open the celebration, foster the unity of those who have been gathered, introduce their thoughts to the mystery of the liturgical time or festivity, and accompany the procession of the Priest and ministers (Article 47).

As a priest, I have been asked this or a similar question multiple times, "How much of Mass can I miss and still have it count?" or "How much of Mass can I miss to miss Mass?" Over the past decades, people have offered various answers to this question. If you are there before the first reading, or you show up before the Gospel, you have fulfilled your obligation. With a touch of humor, I often tell latecomers to Mass who apologize for being late, when I greet them outside, "As long as you are in before the collection, you are good to go." I personally feel these answers are wrong in the context of the aforementioned purpose of the introductory Rite and the need to foster communion and embark on the road together. As I write this page, I am being asked by one of my parishioners to pray for him as he is preparing for a job interview. Isn't it a fact of life that we prepare in advance for a job interview and show up well in advance? What happens if you show up late?

I think it is the responsibility of the Pastor to address tardiness. It is his duty to cultivate in his congregation, in a pastoral way the spiritual discipline that comes from an understanding of the sacredness of the Sacrament and the need to create a spiritual space that allows one to plunge deep into the mystery that is being celebrated. As a priest, I know addressing the issue from the pulpit does not always work, because it often creates a tense dynamic. For some people tardiness is a pattern. They are late to everything: doctor's appointments, to work, to the movies, everything. They will probably be late to their own funeral. For others, there are genuine reasons why they are late—traffic, problem finding a parking space, dealing with children's tantrums just before leaving home, and so much more.

No matter how gently you address the issue, someone out there is going to feel offended or unwelcome or judged by the pastor. Having said that, I would like to ask you, especially if you are one of those who tend to be *habitually* late for Mass, whether it reveals something about your heart in the way you approach worship of God.

We have all been there. Our car broke down. There was an emergency at work. Our ride failed to show up. While arriving late might not be ideal, it does happen to people, and it is sometimes legitimately not your fault. As a rule, however, tardiness has less to do with random faults in the public transport or unexpected emergencies, than a fault in the way we perceive the value of time. I mean other people's time. You can offer a multitude of reasons why you are late, but the overriding reason is that, deep down, you think your time is more valuable than others'. What you forget is that there is always someone on the other side of your thoughtlessness.

I have story for you. After waiting more than an hour and a half for her date, Melissa decided he had stood her up. She changed from her best dinner dress into pajamas and slippers, fixed herself a snack and resigned herself to an evening of TV. No sooner had she slumped down in front of the TV than her doorbell rang. There stood her date. He took one look at her and gasped, "I'm two hours late . . . and you're still not ready?" That relationship was in tatters on many fronts.

Being late for Mass due to legitimate reasons is no big deal in the eyes of God. But, there is a community that expects you to arrive early, and then there is the disruption of a Sacred Liturgy that asks for undivided and shared attention. God is identified with the people gathered in prayer or, as theologians would say, "The Church is the Mystical Body of Christ."

In the words of Joshua Harris, a Pastor in the Covenant Church, a pattern of tardiness reveals something in our souls if we take the gathering of people and worship lightly. Pastor Harris says that, if we are a people of God who thirst for Him, we will be sitting in the front like Mary, the sister of Martha, listening to every word that comes from the Master.

I would ask you to prayerfully consider your attitude towards God and His way of pouring forth grace into your hearts. Harris proposes three "E" words that should describe a Christian's approach to Sunday worship: Eager, Expectant, and Early. We are eager to join our brothers and sisters to sing and pray. This eagerness stems from our desire to be connected to God and to one another. Being expectant demonstrates a faith that God will indeed transform our lives; that He will indeed speak to us through His Word. Because I care, because I deeply thirst and desire God, I will be early. "I would rather have you show up your Sunday looking a bit bedraggled than beautiful and late," says pastor Harris to his congregation (to applause and laughter).

There is no magic when it comes to prayer. Soren Kierkegaard said, "Prayer does not change God, but it changes him who prays." Or, as he might rephrase it, "The function of prayer is not to influence God, but rather to change the nature of the one who prays." In the words of Kierkegaard, it is only superstition to believe that God acts on us only in an external way. God is Spirit. He acts inwardly—upon the inner person. Through prayer, we make it possible for God to enter into our lives and transform us from within. C.S Lewis summarizes it well, "I pray because I can't help myself. I pray because I'm helpless. I pray because the need flows out of me all the time—waking and sleeping. It doesn't change God. It changes me."

I have found this useful in my own personal prayer. There are times when I tend to rush through prayer, something like a function or an obligation. When I remind myself of the words that prayer does not change God, rather it changes me, I slow down and let the words flow from my heart. I often stop at certain phrases or words and let that sink deep.

Eucharistic sacrifice does not change God. He has already paid the price of our salvation. When we allow His Word to enlighten our minds and our hearts, to cast a light on our life situation, change happens.   When we unite ourselves with the sacrifice Jesus accomplished on our behalf, we are loved and forgiven, restored to relationship with God.   When we partake in the fruits of that sacrifice, when we break bread and share the cup in communion, we let God be part of our lives, and we become the One we consume. It changes the nature of the one who partakes of that mystery. God lives in us. He abides in us. The spirit of Jesus lives in us and in our community: "See how they love one another," expressed the change in the first Christian community. An important ingredient of our spirituality is the need to change and change frequently.

As Cardinal Newman put it: "To grow is to change and to have become perfect is to have changed often." Frequent participation in the Eucharistic celebration offers us the opportunity to change frequently, because God speaks to us every time we approach his altar. We are transformed into that which we receive, namely, into the risen Christ.

The question then becomes not how much Mass I can miss to miss Mass. Or, when do I meet the obligation of having participated in Mass? Rather the question becomes, how much do I appreciate Eucharist as an opportunity for change and transformation, an opportunity for God to touch my being from within or as an opportunity to enter into communion with our brothers and sisters? Real change happens in personal or communal behaviors, only when we take time to discover what is worthy of our shared attention. For that to happen, I must be present fully from beginning to end. I must create an ambiance of openness and prayer, so that God may form us according to His will. I must be there early to meet and greet one another in the community, the Mystical Body of Christ. To talk to people I know. Talk to people I don't know. Talk to people I never talk to. As Margaret Wheatley said, "Trust that meaningful conversations can change the world."

Should your parish encourage having a 'stand and greet' time before the procession or the Entrance Hymn?

You know what I am referring to when I address 'stand and greet time' before Mass. In some parishes, this is formalized or even ritualized. "Before we begin our celebration today," a lector might read, "let us take a moment to introduce ourselves to those around us." In the parish I serve right now, the Presider or the deacon informally steps forward and greets and welcomes the congregation, and then asks them to greet the people sitting next to them. Then follows a question they are asked to share. The question is related to the Liturgy of the Word or something that is very pertinent to the day or the feast, or at times is currently critical to them. After sixty seconds or so, the Cantor invites the congregation to stand for the Entrance Hymn. I have read many blogs that express rather strong sentiments, some negative, but not all of them about a "stand and greet" time before Mass.

There are valid issues raised in many parishes by differing groups with regard to this custom. People have listed many reasons why they loathe or love the "stand and greet" time. On one side, people list shyness, insincerity, the awkwardness, nasty hands, and lack of respect for the Sacred as reasons why they don't want their parishes to follow this custom.

On the other side, they say it creates a sense of community and reinforces strong relationships in the Church. Mike Beckner, Pastor of Church that loves this tradition says, "As the pastor I set the

stage and the tone for that time of greeting by what
is said immediately before it . . . It is a great
opportunity to remind people of the need for community and relationship; that we have not gathered
for an insulated and isolated individual experience
but a collective connection with God and each other
as the Body of Christ."

In my parish (I did not start this tradition), by
starting to focus on a question related to the
Liturgy, the congregation now shifts its attention
from things mundane to the sacrament. I would say
this is not a doctrinal issue. It is simply a matter of
preference. You could take it or leave it without
being rude or being perceived as unfriendly. If you
don't want to shake hands, you can just smile. God
loves a cheerful person. Joy is a true mark of a
being a Catholic.

The way we greet each other is an important
part of our heritage, and it reveals a lot about who
we are. Before Mass begins, as their priest I go
around the Church to personally welcome our
parishioners and greet them. Jesus greeted and
welcomed people and conversed with them
wherever he met them. Jesus welcomed children,
while his disciples tried to persuade them to leave.
In the full sight of the apostles, He invited Thomas
to touch Him in the upper room. "Put your finger
here and look at my hands; and put your hand and
place it on my side. Do not disbelieve but believe"
(John 20:27). The Last Supper was in many ways a

deep conversation between Jesus and His apostles that was prefaced with the ritual of washing of the feet. For some of us, it is hard to transition from what we were used to for years to the changes that came about after Vatican II.

If a simple gesture of affection or hospitality before Mass bothers you and if you are one of those who get up and leave the Sacred Enclosure angry, I would ask you to reconsider your decision for the reasons I listed in the previous section about tardiness with regard to Mass. What we celebrate together as a community in the Eucharist transcends personal preferences and dislikes. It is all about unconditional love, communion, reconciliation, and redemption.

One of the passages in Scripture that has helped me grow out of being offended or being angry at faith or Church is the fascinating story of the Syrophoenician woman's encounter with Jesus. She comes to him begging that he cure her daughter of an unclean spirit, something we now know he can easily do. And yet he brushes her off, first giving her the silent treatment, and then refusing her request and casting her aside, throwing in an ethnic slur. Of course, Jesus is testing her faith. The rebuff, the rejection—these are not real at all, but a way of testing to see if she really believed Him. When Jesus says, "It is not good to take the children's bread and throw it to the dogs," do you see what she does? She agrees. She doesn't throw a tantrum or have a fit. She refuses to be offended. She says, "Yes, Lord. But even the dogs feed on the crumbs which fall from their master's table" (Matthew 15:28). What would have happened if she became angry and quit? It would have been the end of the story. She refuses to be offended and pushed back. She is not a passive recipient of God's grace but is determined to participate in what becomes of her life.

Selfishness, hypocrisy, and other 'people problems,' or certain unpersuasive rituals in church can be disappointing. But these shouldn't drive us away from church engagement. Rather, it should make us aware of how much we all need it. It takes courage in life to refuse to be offended. It reveals something about our character and spiritual maturity. Let us not allow anything, especially trivial matters, drive us away from our commu-nities of faith. I am not proposing that we overlook the challenges faced by our parishes or problems associated with liturgical celebrations. We must do what we can to confront them and deal with them in loving ways. It requires patience and love.

The apostle Paul was acutely aware of the inadequacies and imperfections with his Church, yet he wrote: "Bear one another's burdens, and thereby fulfill the law of Christ. For if anyone thinks he is something when he is nothing, he deceives himself. But each one must examine his own work, and then he will have reason for boasting in regard to himself alone, and not in regard to another. For each one will bear his own load" (Galatians 6: 2-5).

So, should parishes that have a "stand and greet" time continue to do so? Is it more negative than positive? Or vice versa? Does your church have this activity? How do you feel about it? I would say it is a good thing to talk about with your spiritual advisor, if you are bothered by this practice. In the spirit of charity, speak to your pastor, letting him know how you feel about it. Remember that it takes courage to refuse to be offended or turned off. In this age of seemingly 'perpetual offense,' one should be careful that our decisions or our opinions do not reveal our own narcissistic preferences or dislikes to the detriment of the community we serve.

I invite parishes and their leaders to revisit these customs and evaluate their benefits for the participating community. Your leaders can set the stage and tone for a meaningful ritual that embraces quiet joyfulness, as well as prayerful conversation before Mass that lends itself to a great celebration.

Liturgy of the Word

The Church has always venerated the divine Scriptures as she venerated the Body of the Lord, in so far as she never ceases, particularly in the sacred liturgy, to partake of the bread of life and to offer it to the faithful from the one table of the Word of God and the Body of Christ. She has always regarded, and continues to regard the Scriptures, taken together with sacred Tradition, as the supreme rule of her faith. . . . In the sacred books the Father who is in heaven comes lovingly to meet his children and talks with them. And such is the force and power of the Word of God that it can serve the Church as her support and vigor, and the children of the Church as strength for their faith, food for the soul, and a pure and lasting foundation of spiritual life (*Divine Revelation*, No. 21).

These words taken from the Second Vatican Council emphasize the supremacy and uniqueness of Sacred Scripture in the celebration of the Holy Eucharist. "When the Scriptures are read in the Church, God himself is speaking to his people and Christ, present in his own word, is proclaiming the Gospel" (GIRM, n. 29). These words unravel the beauty of the celebration of the Liturgy of the Word. The Emmaus story makes it amply clear that Sacred Scripture, when addressed in a given human situation, brings in a new perspective—God's perspective—so much so that the disciples see things in a way they never saw before. God speaks to you directly through Sacred Scripture. God comes to you discernably in His Word. God is equally present in His Word as He is in the Breaking of Bread. In the Eucharist, the baptized are fed from both the table of the Word and the table of the Eucharist. One of the most remarkable statements of Vatican II is that the bishops considered the veneration of the Scriptures on the same level of theological importance as the veneration of the Eucharistic body of Jesus.

I would like to share with you a story told by Anthony De Mello, a 20th Century Jesuit priest from India. This story about a villager and the *sannyasi* (a holy person, who in the Indian spiritual tradition, has renounced worldly goods and interests to focus on the spiritual search) has much to say to us about how God speaks in mysterious ways, leading to change and transformation:

> The sannyasi had reached the outskirts of the village and settled down under a tree for the night when a villager came running up to him and said, "The stone! The stone! Give me the precious stone!"
> "What stone?" asked the sannyasi.

"Last night the Lord Shiva (one of the main gods of the Hindu religion) appeared to me in a dream," said the villager, "and told me that if I went to the outskirts of the village at dusk I should find a sannyasi who would give me a precious stone that would make me rich forever."

The sannyasi rummaged in his bag and pulled out a stone. "He probably meant this one," he said, as he handed the stone over to the villager. "I found it on a forest path some days ago. You can certainly have it."

The man gazed at the stone in wonder. It was a diamond, probably the largest diamond in the whole world, for it was as large as a person's head. He took the diamond and walked away. All night he tossed about in bed, unable to sleep. Next day at the crack of dawn, he woke the sannyasi and said, "Give me the wealth that makes it possible for you to give this stone away."

In the letter to the Hebrews, St. Paul asserts, "For the word of God is living and active and sharper than any two-edged sword and piercing as far as the division of soul and spirit, of both joints and marrow, and able to judge the thoughts and intentions of the heart" (Hebrews 4:12). When we listen to the Word of God, with a genuine desire to know it and know Him, we cannot escape conviction. The phrase, "able to judge the thoughts and intentions of the heart," speaks to conversion that accompanies the Word being proclaimed. The crestfallen disciples, whose hearts were full of hopelessness and sorrow on the road to Emmaus, experienced a burning sensation, as they heard the stranger enlighten them with quote after quote from Sacred Scripture. They were restored to wholeness. The Word of God, who is a person, takes what you are and what you have and gives you what He is and what He has. He offers fullness never experience before.

In speaking directly to the villager, Lord Shiva was already aware of the thoughts and intentions that filled his heart. The villager directed his energies towards gaining the material wealth so prized by society, but the sannyasi had gained his wealth by emptying himself of those desires, by becoming poor in that sense. It was a paradox the world could not understand. Lord Shiva directed the villager to a holy man free from those human drives which make us want, accumulate and, resort to any means to achieve wealth. That encounter resulted in the villager receiving the grace of conversion. He no longer wanted material wealth, but only the wealth that came from the ability to give away some unfathomable treasure.

This wealth, deeply rooted in poverty of Spirit, is now dependent totally on God, and God will never fail. Saint Augustine, from his own experience of conversion, summarized it this way: "You have made us for yourself, O God, and our hearts are restless until they rest in You." Like the woman of Samaria, assured by Jesus that she would never be thirsty again, the villager would never hunger for material possessions, because he had listened to his God and the Word of God, which was alive and active and pierced the innermost recesses of his heart, bringing wholeness.

The Word of God, a Person, completely takes over the one who is devoted to the Word. It cleanses and purifies. It leads to fullness. The Word of God keeps you on the Way of righteousness. "How can the young keep his way without fault? Only by observing your words" (Psalm 119).

We Catholics do not come to Mass for a Scripture study. *The Catechism of the Catholic Church* states, "The liturgical Word and action are inseparable both insofar as they are signs and instruction and insofar as they accomplish what they signify. When the Holy Spirit awakens faith, he not only gives an understanding of the Word of God, but through the sacraments also makes present the 'wonders' of God which it proclaims. The Spirit makes present and communicates the Father's work, fulfilled by the beloved Son."

In the Eucharistic celebration, the Liturgy of the Word not only penetrates the innermost recesses of your being, but God opens your eyes of faith and awakens a whole set of spiritual senses, so you can recognize Jesus fully in the breaking of the bread. Beyond the color, taste and shape, you know and believe in your heart that it truly is the Body and Blood of Christ. Every fiber of your body, all the senses of your being, now illumined and enlightened by the Word that is addressed to you, see the Eucharistic mystery from His point of view. Jesus gives Himself to us. With His Word, Jesus (the stranger) allowed the disheartened and confused disciples to enter into the history of Salvation, promised through the Prophets, and to behold the recent events in Jerusalem as the 'doings' of God and eventually recognize the Messiah.

As you listen to Jesus through the Liturgy of the Word, the same Jesus opens your eyes of faith to behold the 'doings' of God and enter into the history of salvation enacted here and now and recognize the Messiah, who died and gave himself up to us in his Body and Blood.

For this reason, *The Catechism of the Catholic Church* states:

The Liturgy of the Word is an integral part of sacramental celebrations. To nourish the faith of believers, the signs which accompany the Word of God should be emphasized: the book of the Word (a Lectionary or a Book of the Gospels), its veneration (procession, incense, candles), the place of its proclamation (lectern or ambo), its audible and intelligible reading, the minister's homily which extends its proclamation, and the responses of the assembly (acclamations, meditation psalms, litanies, and profession of faith).

The *General Introduction to the Lectionary* goes as far as to say, "The church has honored the word of God and the Eucharistic mystery with the same reverence, although not with the same worship, and has always and everywhere insisted upon and sanctioned such honor."

Let us look at some of the signs that accompany the Liturgy of the Word of God.

1. Ambo

"The dignity of the Word of God requires the church to have a suitable place for announcing his message so that the attention of the people may be easily directed to that place during the liturgy of the Word" (*Catechism of the Catholic Church*).

The ambo, 'the altar of His Word' is the place that houses the Sacred Scripture and accommodates the Celebrant, who stands *in persona Christi*, as well as the Lectors who proclaim the Word. It should be a fixed and dignified place that parallels the altar itself. In the words of Fr. David J. Dohogne, "While the Scriptures have always played an important role in the liturgical celebrations of the Church, the use of the ambo gives us a renewed appreciation and a deeper understanding of the importance and necessity of God's Word in our lives. As a sacred furnishing of the church which complements the altar, the ambo should be constructed of quality materials and beautifully designed, giving it the dignity it deserves."

2. The Book of the Gospel and the Lectionary, procession, candles, and incense

Two books are used during the Eucharistic celebration for the Liturgy of the Word—the Lectionary and the Book of the Gospels. A Lectionary contains all the Scripture readings, including the Gospel. The Book of the Gospels contains only the Gospel readings. Its dimensions are usually larger than the Lectionary to give it some added dignity and set the Gospel apart. In some parishes, they use a rich and beautifully decorated cover to emphasize the greatness of the Word. The Lectionary is placed on the Ambo in preparation for the Mass.

During the entrance procession, the deacon carries the book of the Gospels. If a deacon is not present, one of the Lectors should carry the Book of the Gospels in an elevated position for all to witness and revere. It is then placed on the altar, as a sign that Jesus is already present in the Word, especially in the Gospel, where we listen to his own words.

After the second reading, the Book of the Gospels is again carried in procession from the altar to the Ambo by the deacon or the priest, accompanied by candle bearers and incense. I have heard comments from members of our Liturgical

Committee questioning the need for the Book of the Gospels, when the Lectionary already contains the Gospel reading.

As a priest, I have been tempted to read from the Lectionary as a matter of convenience. According to Fr. Paul Turner, "So much happens at the moment the Gospel is proclaimed—greeting, kissing, crossing, incensing, standing, etc.—that only in slow motion can we really appreciate it for what it really is: not just another Word of God, but the 'Good News,' spoken from the lips of Jesus, the incarnate Word of God."

The Gospel reading is prefaced with a greeting, "The Lord be with you," to which the assembly responds, "And with your Spirit." Once again, as the congregation professed their faith at the start of the Eucharistic celebration, at this moment in the Liturgy of the Word, the assembly professes that Christ personally ministers through the deacon or the priest in such a way that the words we hear are indeed from the lips of the Master himself.

The deacon or priest then makes the **sign of the cross** on the book, then on his forehead, lips, and heart. The congregation does the same. This profound gesture of faith is an act of prayer that the Word of God, "alive and active, sharper than any double-edged sword" (Hebrews 4:12) may pierce our mind, lips, and hearts. The gesture signifies that we want to hear the Gospel with an open mind, proclaim it with our lips, and treasure it in our hearts just as our Blessed Mother Mary cherished the Word in her heart.

We cross our forehead so that the Word of God may be in our thoughts and purify our minds. We cross our lips, so the Word may sanctify our speech and persuade us to witness the Gospel with courage and conviction. And we cross our hearts to invite God to transform our lives through our acceptance and obedience.

There are prayers the deacon or the priest says silently to himself before and after proclaiming the Gospel, which reminds him of the significance of what he is about to do and bestows on him the dignity and power concomitant with the proclamation of the Good News. Before the Gospel reading, the priest or the deacon bows before the altar and silently prays: "Almighty God, cleanse my heart and my lips that I may worthily proclaim Your Gospel."

After the Gospel, he kisses the Gospel Book and prays: "May the words of the Gospel wipe away our sins." Pope Benedict said, "The silent prayers of the priest invite him to make his task truly personal, so that he may give his whole self to the Lord. . . . These priestly prayers . . . do exist—they have to exist, now as before."

Our everyday awareness of God comes to us through our senses: sight, sound, smell, touch, and taste. They are the pathways to the deepest parts of our imagination and understanding. "Faith opens a window to the presence and working of the Spirit," says Pope Francis. The signs and gestures, posture and prayers before, during and after the Gospel reading signify proper disposition, reverence, adoration and praise. Furthermore, they engage the totality of our being—body, mind, and spirit—in the act of worship. In the Liturgy of the Word, in particular, they awaken our spiritual senses to receive the Word with joy and cherish it deeply in our souls. It is a fact of life that devoutness is always tied to some gestures, and they enrich the spiritual soil to bear abundant fruit.

Lectors

The Church treasures the gifts, talents and faith of the laity. It incorporates them in various aspects of the Church's life and mission, prayer and worship. Lectors or Readers are those commissioned to read the Scripture during the Eucharistic celebration. They are part of a tradition going back to Old Testament times, when religious leaders allowed people to read the Scriptures in public. Moses, towards the end of his life, instructed the leaders to read the law and learn it, and thus to fear the Lord: "Assemble the people, men, women and children as well as aliens—that they may hear the law and learn it and so fear the Lord, your God, and carefully observe all the words of the law" (Deut. 31:12).

At the outset of his public ministry, Jesus went to the synagogue in Nazareth and read the Scripture passage that related to him: "He stood up to read; and there was given to him the book of the prophet Isaiah. He opened the book and found the place where it was written: 'The Spirit of the Lord is upon me, because he has anointed me to preach good news to the poor'" (Luke. 4: 16). In the words of Peter Schineller, "Jesus, known simply as the son of Joseph to the people of Nazareth, was a layperson, not a priest or Levite, not a Scribe. As a lay reader in the synagogue he proclaims the word of God from the Old Testament—the prophet Isaiah. He read very well, because it says, "The eyes of all in the synagogue looked intently at him" (Luke. 4:20). Then, Jesus said to them: 'Today this scripture passage is fulfilled in your hearing" (v. 21).

Lectors today proclaim the Word of God from the Ambo with reverence and joy, because they are called to this life-giving ministry, thanks to the God-given gift of public speaking and integrity of life. Pope Paul VI describes the role and ministry of Lectors in *Ministeria Quaedam,* reminding them that they are indeed disciples of the Lord:

He should meditate assiduously on the sacred scriptures so that he may more fittingly and perfectly fulfill these functions. The lector should be mindful of the office he has undertaken and should do all in his power to acquire increasingly that sweet and living love and knowledge of the scriptures that will make him a more perfect disciple of the Lord.

Fr. Schineller expanded the words of Pope Paul VI, "All Christians are called to be disciples of Christ, but lectors, commissioned to proclaim the Scriptures in the Church, are called in a very special way to follow Jesus Christ, the Word of God made flesh. Thus, the ministry of lector is a gift and a task. It is a privilege that also involves responsibility and disciplined training." The words of Pope Francis in *Joy of the Gospel* should inspire Lectors in their study and meditation of the Word of God: "When we stop and attempt to understand the message of a particular text, we are practicing reverence for the truth. It's the humility of heart which recognizes that the word of God is always beyond us, that we are neither its masters or owners, but its guardians, heralds and servants."

Unlike the priests, deacon and altar servers, Lectors are not required to wear certain prescribed vestments. However, the dignity of the Sacred Liturgy and the sacred nature of their commission require those ministering as Lectors to dress in a reverent and appropriate manner. Preparation is key to fulfilling this awesome ministry.

Cardinal Roger Mahoney expressed it this way: "Parish lectors will be effective in proclaiming the Word of God in the liturgy in the measure they meditate upon it beforehand." When you are assigned to proclaim the Word of God to the community, prepare by reading aloud and studying the passage in the days leading up to the cele-bration.

Lector workbooks are helpful for this preparation. In my current parish assignment, it is mandatory for Lectors to gather in the church for a Saturday morning of prayer, study, and practice of the reading. The Coordinator of the ministry or someone assigned by him gives a touch of context to the readings, so that the Lectors can communicate to the assembly the way the Word of God was first addressed. Different materials entail different treatment. Fr. Schineller explained it well:

Thus, you read the theological part of a letter of Paul as if you were conducting an argument. One reads Sirach or Wisdom or much of the Gospel of Matthew (Sermon on the Mount) to bring out individual wise sayings. One should read the strong words of the prophets with power, as if you are the prophet speaking to his people One reads the love poetry of some of the Psalms with passion. If it is a Psalm of praise or joy, show you are joyful, excited too. In general, note that the Psalms are poetry, and so the style and rhythm of reading the psalm is different from reading a story of freedom or liberation from the book of Exodus. Read the laws as if you are a lawgiver, with a clear, no-nonsense voice.

A Lector once remarked to me that listening to his colleagues practice the same passage enabled him to be a better reader. He learned to vary vocal pace, tone and volume. Sometimes your colleagues will give you constructive feedback that would improve your reading skills significantly. Another good idea is to record yourself, if you can stand listening to yourself, because it is one of the only ways to be objective about your own pacing, style, tone and all the other things that go with reading in public.

Lectors should arrive ahead of time, so they can enter into a spirit of prayer before the Liturgy commences. It is important to make sure that the Lectionary is correctly marked and placed on the Ambo well in advance. If Lectors are part of the entrance procession, they should be at the entrance of the Church, ready and prepared for the procession. The lector may never change the words of a reading or proclaim from a non-scripture text during Mass (GIRM 57).

Liturgy of the Word—Structure

Most of the Liturgy of the Word is made up of readings from Sacred Scripture. On Sundays and solemnities, there are three Scripture readings. During most of the year, the first reading is from the Old Testament and the second reading is from one of the New Testament letters. During Easter Time, the first reading is taken from the Acts of the Apostles, which tells the story of the Church's earliest days. The last reading is always taken from one of the four Gospels. There is continuity between the three readings as well as the responsorial Psalm, which indicates that the plan of God to save the world existed from the beginning.

A moment of silence is recommended at the end of each of the Scripture reading before and after the concluding refrains, "The Word of the Lord" and "Thanks be to God." Msgr. Guido Marini, Master of Pontifical Ceremonies, described the meaning of this silence beautifully with these words:

A well-celebrated liturgy, in its different parts, plans a happy alteration of silence and speech, in which silence animates speech, allows the voice to resonate with an extraordinary depth, and keeps each verbal expression in the right atmosphere of recollection. . . . The required silence must not . . . be considered as a pause between one moment in the celebration and the next. Rather, it should be considered as a true moment of the ritual, complementing the words, the vocal prayer, the song, and the gestures.

Let us look at the structure of the celebration of the Liturgy of the Word. Some of the information given below is adapted from All Saints Parish in Mesa, Arizona.

1. The First Reading

The first reading is mostly chosen from the Old Testament. During the Easter season, the Book of Acts is read. During some solemnities (All Saints and Immaculate Conception), the book of Revelation is proclaimed. The first reading is always linked in some way to the Gospel. It highlights the Gospel in one of many ways: (a) to show how a prophecy in the Old Testament is fulfilled through Jesus Christ in the Gospel; (b) to make a contrast between events and personalities in the Old Testament and the Gospel; (c) to make the meaning of the Gospel clearer through giving the rest of the story.

2. The Responsorial Psalm

The Psalm reflects themes in the readings. It serves as the response of the congregation to the reading they have just heard. An antiphon accompanies the Psalm and is a vehicle of prayer and praise. The psalms were selected with utmost care. Furthermore, psalms having a connection with a particular liturgical season are used during that season, e.g. the penitential psalms during Lent.

It is strongly recommended that we sing the psalm as a community, led by a cantor from the Ambo. "The reason is threefold: the genre of the psalms as lyrical compositions calls for singing; the psalm is a response to the spoken word and ritual structure does not customarily respond to speech with more speech; this is the only time in the liturgy when a psalm is used for its own sake and not to accompany a ritual action. Every effort, therefore, is to be made to sing the psalm response" (Sunday Bulletin, St. Paul Roman Catholic Cathedral, Saskatoon, SK, Canada; April 27, 2008).

3. The Second Reading

The Second Reading is usually from a letter written by one of the apostles, most notably St Paul. During Eastertime, we read from the Book of Revelation.

4. Gospel Acclamation

The Gospel acclamation heralds the Gospel with a song of praise. The priest or deacon goes to the altar where the Gospel is enthroned and lifts the book. Accompanied by altar servers with candles and on some occasions incense (symbols of Christ's light), processes with the Gospel Book held high, while the choir and community acclaim the good news with the Acclamation. During most of the year, the congregation sings, "Alleluia" ("praise to God"), alternating with verses appropriate to the Gospel.

During Lent, another acclamation is substituted since 'Alleluia' is seen as too joyful to be sung during the season of Lent. The Gospel Acclamation should be sung, not recited.

5. The Gospel Reading

The Gospel is the climax of the Liturgy of the

Word. Gospel means "Good News." What we hear proclaimed at Mass truly is Good News—the best news we can hear: Jesus Christ speaks to us! It is important to remember that, when the Gospel is proclaimed, it is no longer the priest or deacon speaking, but Christ himself. We should pay especially close attention to the words of the Gospel as they are proclaimed.

To help us focus on this important reading, the Church provides some additional postures and symbols of respect. First, we stand out of respect for the Gospel reading. Second, the Gospel is often in a special book, the Book of Gospels, that has a place of honor during the Mass. Incense and candles are used on solemn feasts to emphasize that Christ is present, speaking to us through the Gospel we hear.

It has become a custom for one to make a small sign of the cross on the forehead, lips, and heart before the proclamation of the Gospel. Originally, this gesture belonged only to the deacon or priest proclaiming the Gospel, and only when the bishop celebrated the Mass. Over time, priests and deacons began to use this gesture at all Masses. The laity adopted the same gesture.

Even though this gesture has been in use for centuries, there were no regulations requiring this gesture at Mass until the 1980s!

When you make this gesture, ask God to bless your mind, that you may ponder his Word; your lips, that you may speak his praise; and your heart, that you may love the Word of God! Catholic faith teaches that in proclaiming the Gospel, Christ is truly present to the community. For this reason, the community stands in witness to Christ's resurrection, which allows him to be present to his people.

6. The Homily

St. Paul wrote, "Faith comes through preaching" (Rom 3: 13-15). He underscored the importance of preaching again in his Second Letter to Timothy 4: 2b-5:

> Preach the word; be prepared in season and out of season; correct, rebuke and encourage—with great patience and careful instruction. For the time will come when people will not put up with sound doctrine. Instead, to suit their own desires, they will gather around them a great number of teachers to say what their itching ears want to hear. They will turn their ears away from the truth and turn aside to myths. But you, keep your head in all situations, endure hardship, do the work of an evangelist, discharge all the duties of your ministry." From this perspective, Paul understood preaching as an antidote to falsehood and heresy.

Preaching is rooted in the Jewish belief that the creative power of God's word transforms human life. The Scriptures are not always easy to understand and apply to present life. For this reason, the homily breaks open the Scriptures, showing how the word of God addresses us today. What import does the Gospel have for our lives today, for the world we live in, for issues in the community forum?

Pope Francis in his Apostolic Exhortation, *Evangelii Gaudium*, has this great message for priests:

> We know that the faithful attach great importance to [the homily] and that both they and their ordained ministers suffer because of homilies: the laity from having to listen to them and the clergy from having to preach them! It is sad that this is the case. The homily can actually be an intense and happy experience of the Spirit, a consoling encounter with God's word, a constant source of renewal and growth (No. 135).

According to the pope, a homily is "a dialogue between God and his people, a dialogue in which the great deeds of salvation are proclaimed, and the demands of the covenant are continually restated" (No. 132).

7. The Creed (Profession of Faith)

After the Homily on most Sundays and Holy Days, we stand and recite the Creed. The creed that we pray at Mass originated in Jerusalem as a profession of faith before baptism. This was formalized in 325 C.E. at the Council of Nicaea and further developed at the Council of Constantinople in 381. This creed is known as the Nicene-Constantinople Creed, or more commonly as the Nicene Creed. Its opening words are, "I believe in God." Pope Benedict XVI had this to say about the Creed:

It is a fundamental affirmation, seemingly simple in its essence, but it opens on to the infinite world of the relationship with the Lord and with his mystery. Believing in God entails adherence to him, the acceptance of his word and joyful obedience to his revelation." The structure of the creed reinforces our belief in the Holy Trinity, first addressing the Father, then the Son, and then the Holy Spirit, stressing that the three persons are one God. At the heart of our faith is our belief that God became one of us at the birth of Christ. To highlight our belief in this truth, we are asked to bow at the words "By the power of the Holy Spirit, he was born of the Virgin Mary, and became man.

On Easter Sunday or on Sundays when we have baptisms, we are asked to renew our baptismal promises. We are asked about our belief, to which we respond, "I do," to each statement of our faith.

The renewal of our baptismal promises is also a creed, a statement of belief, based on the Apostles Creed.

The creed is a statement of the truths, which we hold as Catholics. When we recite this prayer together, we express not only our individual belief, but also the faith which all of us hold in common. We return to these familiar "words of faith" week after week to remind and refocus ourselves on the truth. The creed is a very important prayer! When we pray it together, be sure to join in. You may even want to memorize the prayer to make it truly your own!

8. Prayers of the Faithful

The Prayers of the Faithful, also known as the General Intercessions or Universal Prayers, take place at the conclusion of the Liturgy of the Word, and serve as a hinge connecting the Liturgy of the Word to the Liturgy of the Eucharist (the next part of the Mass). The structure of the prayers of the faithful is generally the same: a short introduction by the priest, followed by multiple intercessions proclaimed by a deacon or lector, and a short concluding prayer led by the priest. At the end of each petition, we offer a response, such as, "Lord, hear our prayer."

While there are no official texts for the prayers of the faithful, they follow a general order: For the needs of the Church, for public authorities and the salvation of the world; for those burdened with any kind of difficulty; for the local community, etc. Writing the prayers of the faithful has been described as having "a Bible in one hand and a newspaper in the other," drawing parallels between the readings proclaimed at Mass and current events for which we should pray today. At some Masses, the deacon or priest will also include a moment of silence allowing the congregation to pray for their own personal intentions.

The prayers of the faithful truly belong to the faithful, that is, to all who are baptized. This is a time not just for those needs close to us as individuals, but also for the needs of the parish, the diocese, the country, and for the Church as a whole. When we pray in this way, we recognize our place within the larger community of the baptized, and bring those prayers and intentions with us as we move forward in the Mass.

I would like to add a favorite quote of mine, attributed to the Dutch evangelist and spiritual writer Corrie ten Boom: "We never know how God will answer our prayers, but we can expect that He will get us involved in His plan for the answer. If we are true intercessors, we must be ready to take part in God's work on behalf of the people for whom we pray."

Recommendations for a Fruitful Celebration of the Liturgy of the Word

At all times, preparation is key to a meaningful

celebration of Liturgy. This is truer, when it comes to participation in the Liturgy of the Word, which consists mostly of words and speech. At times, Scripture Readings transport us to unfamiliar territories. A preacher noticed that a man had fallen asleep and was snoring loudly, so he interrupted his sermon to ask the man's wife to wake him up. She answered indignantly, "You're the one who put him to sleep, so you wake him up!" Well, we are all too familiar with that in our own lives. How many of us have slept through an entire Mass? It takes a heroic effort to keep our minds from wandering away from the most important mystery unfolding before us in the Liturgy of the Word. If you have children with you, you will need to double or triple your efforts at attentiveness. Therefore, careful planning, coordination and good delivery on the part of the ministers of the Word becomes imperative.

The sound system in the church is an important aspect of worship. Regardless of the size of your sanctuary, a sound system that allows the Word and the music to be heard with detail and clarity at the appropriate level for the congregation, based on the style, culture, and makeup of your church, should be a high priority. Priests, deacons, lectors and cantors should be familiar with the use of microphones in the church and should rehearse their parts in the church, using the sound system.

Richard McKinley, Managing Director of Contacta, Inc., a maker of hearing assist technology, points out that quite a few worshippers with hearing aids—as many as half or more—simply stop attending church if they can't hear the sermon. "A church wouldn't keep wheelchair users from attending worship services, but there are 15 times as many hearing aid wearers who don't have access," he asserts.

Though Churches are exempt from the requirement of having an assistive listening system, it is only pastoral to accommodate parishioners with hearing impairment. Pastors should invite members with hearing problems to use the technology provided by their church.

The great thing about the Liturgy of the Word is that you can look the readings up ahead of time. You can read them in a missalette or online. Some sites provide useful background information to better understand the upcoming Sunday's readings.

In our parish, multiple groups come together before Sunday to read the texts together, to gain an appreciation for the context and then share their personal insights with one another. This hour spent fruitfully in an intimate setting of love and prayer contributes to the active and attentive participation with the Christian community on Sunday. Some of the groups meet in the parish facilities, while others meet in homes, creating a sacred space where true learning and growth can take place.

To use the pedagogy of Parker Palmer, this learning and growing space should ensure three essential dimensions: openness, boundaries, and an air of hospitality. This sacred space should be open to the many paths down which discovery may take us. It needs to be hospitable, inviting as well as open, safe and trustworthy, as well as free. It must respect the voice of the individual and revere the voice of the group. Individuals need the freedom to express themselves, their thoughts, and feelings. It is paramount that this space creates room for personal stories and experiences and the group should be able to explore ways in which they fit in with others and relate to the larger story of the readings. From a deeply spiritual side, the study should integrate silence that enables an opportunity to reflect, a silence that leads to interiorization of the truths that we have heard and received.

I personally participated in one of the groups consisting of 8-10 workingmen who met every Wednesday from 6:30 a.m. to 7:30 a.m. I can only praise God for the spiritual growth and transformation I have witnessed in the last ten years. The disciples hid behind closed doors for fear. Then, reenergized by the Risen Lord, they went everywhere proclaiming the Good News. The committed men in that group have moved further in their faith. The men I met with have engaged themselves in multiple ministries, from confirmation teachers to organizing and leading larger ministries, such as Catholics at Work and Family Aid to Catholic Education. One of them registered himself for deaconate formation.

The temptation for many groups that come

together is to become Coffee Shop Churches that require little commitment, no preparation, and absolutely no ownership. These don't flourish and grow. I recommend that you create similar small communities based on Sunday Scriptures, because Jesus walks with you on your journey to the New Emmaus and interacts with you as you confront your daily struggles and tussle with everyday decisions. Before you know it, you too will be spiritually charged and sanctified during your week.

Cantors or psalmists play a vital role in the Liturgy of the Word. They lead the congregation in proclaiming in song the Responsorial Psalm, as well as welcoming the Good News of the Gospel with the rendering of the Alleluia or its equivalent during the season of Lent. In the Liturgy of the Word, which is predominantly speech driven, beautifully singing the Psalm engages the assembly more deeply—heart, mind, soul, and strength.

The responsorial Psalm is an integral part of the Liturgy of the Word. It should be sung from the Ambo with reverence and love. "As one who proclaims the Word, the psalmist should be able to proclaim the text of the Psalm with clarity, conviction, and sensitivity to the text, the music setting, and those who are listening" (GIRM 35). In the proclamation of the Psalm, it is important to give more emphasis to the text being proclaimed than to the musical setting of the text, so that the congregation may receive the Word intelligibly.

Kathleen Harmon, music director for programs of
the Institute for Liturgical Ministry, asks cantors or
psalmists to be sensitive to the text of the Psalm:

> The psalmist needs to know the type of text
> the psalm is (that is, a lament, a hymn of
> praise, a song of ascents, a royal psalm, etc.)
> and how its genre shapes its content and
> images and colors its words. More
> importantly, he or she must understand the
> relationship between the psalm text and the
> readings of the day to which it is juxtaposed.
> Within the context of this particular Liturgy
> of the Word, the psalm is meant to lead the
> assembly to a Paschal Mystery encounter
> with Christ in the Gospel reading. It is the
> psalmist's role to lead the assembly to this
> encounter; to do so, he or she must have
> already walked this journey.

The psalmist should also be sensitive to the
assembly, who are listening and engaged in singing
with the psalmist. The psalmist engages in a
personal encounter with God through the words of
the psalm. The challenge is to transfer that personal
encounter into a shared encounter of the assembly
with God. For this to happen, the Church must
provide training for the ministry of the psalmist.
Harmon underscored the need for training, stating:
"The psalmist needs to have a broad knowledge of
the psalms and their history, their genres, and their

spirituality. The psalmist needs to understand how Christ is the messianic fulfillment of the psalms, how the psalms are the prayer of Christ and consequently of the Church."

In selecting psalmists, music directors should not only pay attention to their voice, but also to their liturgical awareness and spirituality. *The Introduction to the Lectionary for Mass* identifies the psalm as a song. Even when not sung, it is to be "recited in a manner conducive to meditation on the word of God."

Liturgy of the Eucharist

The Liturgy of the Word nourishes us through Sacred Scripture. It awakens our spiritual senses— opens our eyes of faith to witness the Eucharistic miracle. The Liturgy of the Eucharist commences with the preparation of the gifts and the altar. In this preparation, traditionally called the Offertory, the celebrant prepares the gifts to be offered. Many things occur simultaneously: the preparation of the gifts, preparation of the altar, the collection, and the offertory hymn. As the deacon and other ministers prepare the altar, representatives from the assembly bring up bread and wine, which will become the body and blood of our Lord Jesus Christ. The celebrant will bless and offer the gifts to Lord, and then place them on the altar. The offertory prayer concludes the preparation of the gifts and the altar. Let us look at each of the offerings, prayers, and rituals in detail.

The Gifts of Bread and Wine

In 2004, the story of Haley Waldman caught the attention of a lot of people, including the secular media. According to *The New York Times*:

Haley Waldman, 8 years old, with stringy brown hair and a sensitive stomach, comes from a Roman Catholic family, and her mother is on a quest for her to take Holy Communion the same way as any other Catholic girl. But Haley cannot eat wheat. She suffers from celiac disease, an obscure but increasingly diagnosed condition that strikes the small intestine, and even the trace amount of wheat in the communion wafer, or host, can make her ill. So, she and her mother, who live in Brielle, on the Jersey Shore about 60 miles south of Manhattan, are asking the Catholic Church to make an exception. They want a wafer without wheat. They even tracked down a Seattle company that bakes special wheat-free communion wafers that several other Christian denominations, like Methodists and Episcopalians, allow. Haley's quest has reached all the way up to the Vatican, reverberating in parishes, on talk radio and in newspaper columns, and rallying various groups of celiac sufferers to the third grader's side.

The Times stated that the Church was not budging. "Bread, to be valid matter for the Eucharist, must be made solely of wheat," said a statement issued by their diocese on behalf of the Catholic Church. "This is not an issue to be determined at the diocesan or parish level but has already been decided for the Roman Catholic Church throughout the world by Vatican authority." We need to look at the use of Bread and Wine in the Holy Sacrifice of the Mass.

During the Last Supper, which Jesus celebrated in the context of the Passover, He definitely used unleavened wheat bread and grape wine. From its inception, the Church has never deviated from this tradition. The *Code of Canon Law* (Canon 924) mandates: "The Most Sacred Eucharistic Sacrifice must be celebrated with bread and wine, with which a small quantity of water is to be mixed. The bread must be made of wheat alone, recently made so that there is no danger of corruption. The wine must be natural wine of the grape and not corrupt."

Why did our Lord use bread and wine as elements of his memorial? Archbishop Fulton J. Sheen answered this question, and I would like you to understand his account unfiltered.

First of all, because no two substances in nature better symbolize unity than bread and wine. As bread is made from a multiplicity of grains of wheat, and wine is made from a multiplicity of grapes, so the many who believe are one in Christ. Second, no two substances in nature have to suffer more to become what they are than bread and wine. Wheat has to pass through the rigors of winter, be ground beneath the Calvary of a mill, and then subjected to purging fire before it can become bread. Grapes in their turn must be subjected to the Gethsemane of a wine press and have their life crushed from them to become wine. Thus do they symbolize the Passion and Sufferings of Christ, and the condition of Salvation, for Our Lord said unless we die to ourselves we cannot live in Him. A third reason is that there are no two substances in nature, which have more traditionally nourished man than bread and wine. In bringing these elements to the altar, men are equivalently bringing themselves. When bread and wine are taken or consumed, they are changed into man's body and blood. But when He took bread and wine, He changed them into Himself.

Cardinal Telesphore Toppo, addressing the theme, *Eucharist and Mission*, told the assembly, "The bread and wine that they bring to the altar is the symbol of their daily life of interaction with one another. They are not mere ritual elements. They represent the community with its life of relationships. In the early Church these were taken from the table of sharing and thus expressed their relationship among themselves." He went on to emphasize the social and communitarian dimension of the bread and wine that is brought to the altar. It was such an understanding of the Eucharist, which made St. Paul critical of the abuses and division creeping in among the Corinthians, even in those early days, and corrupting their memorial of the Lord's Supper. He wanted the Eucharist to be a real sharing in mind and goods and, therefore, he says that the Eucharistic community is to form one body: "Is not the bread which we break a sharing in the body of Christ? Since there is one bread, we who are many are one body; for we all partake of the one bread" (1 Cor. 10: 16 – 17).

St. Augustine, in one of his sermons, empha-sized the bond and unity of believers in sharing the cup: "Many grapes hang in the cluster, but the liquid of the grapes is mixed in unity. So also did Christ the Lord portray us. He willed that we belong to Him. He consecrated the mystery of our peace and unity upon His table. He who receives the mystery of unity and does not hold fast to the bond of peace, receives not a mystery for himself, but testimony against himself." In short, Eucharistic participation leads to the building of "one mind, one heart" (Acts 4: 32) toward God.

Celiac Disease, Alcohol Intolerance—
The Church's Pastoral Response

So, what can Haley Waldman do about com-munion? What alternatives are available to her? Anyone who is allergic to the gluten in wheat could make her first Holy Communion by receiving the Precious Blood from the chalice. Jesus is truly and fully present and given by receiving just the sacred

host, or just the Precious Blood, or both. A number
of convents of religious sisters, who make the hosts,
have started making wheat hosts in which gluten
has been almost completely removed. USCCB has
given clear guidelines on this matter. The conference states, "It might be necessary for someone
who has permission to receive Holy Communion
under the species of wine alone to prepare before
Mass a chalice, which will not be part of the
commingling rite and from which either they alone
will receive or from which they will be the first to
receive. Such precautions are not only medically
necessary, but they demonstrate compassion to
avoid singling out those who want to receive
Communion but are unable to receive one or the
other species." The document requests the parishes
to accommodate those who cannot receive bread
under any circumstances, "The lay faithful who are
not able to receive Holy Communion at all under
the species of bread, even of low-gluten hosts, may
receive Holy Communion under the species of wine
only, regardless of whether the Precious Blood is
offered to the rest of the faithful present at a given
celebration of Mass."

In 2003, the Congregation for the Doctrine of the
Faith set forth new norms which assign authority to
the local ordinary to grant permission for priests,
deacons, or lay persons to receive Communion
under the matter of *mustum* (grape juice), as well as
low gluten hosts. With the approval of these norms,
a person who is gluten or alcohol intolerant should

be able to make arrangements with the pastor to have low-gluten hosts or *mustum* present. The use of these alternatives is reserved to those who need them. For example, if a person can only receive Communion under the matter of *mustum*, the priest will consecrate a separate chalice for that person along with the customary bread and wine for the rest of the congregation.

The Altar in the Catholic Liturgy

The *General Instruction on the Roman Missal* stated, "The altar on which the Sacrifice of the Cross is made present under sacramental signs is also the table of the Lord to which the People of God are called together to participate in the Mass, as well as the center of the thanksgiving that is accomplished through the Eucharist" (296). Thus, for us Catholics the altar is a sacrificial table as well as a table for a common meal. During the celebration of Mass, the altar occupies a preeminent place in the sanctuary. That is why you see the celebrants kiss the altar during the entrance procession and the conclusion of Mass. In kissing the altar, the priest honors and reveres the altar of sacrifice, which represents Christ, where the Eucharistic miracle takes place. There is another reason for this act of reverence, which is rooted in ancient Christian tradition: to reverence the relics of the saint or martyr placed within the altar itself.

During the first centuries when Christianity was illegal, Masses were celebrated in the underground catacombs on stone slabs covering the tomb of a martyr. When Emperor Constantine legalized Christianity in early 4th Century, the celebration of the Eucharist moved from the catacombs to churches or public buildings. During this transition, churches were built over the tombs of martyrs. The basilicas of St. Peter and St. Paul in Rome are examples of this. When this was not possible, they placed a stone slab containing the relic of a saint or martyr on top of the altar. During the Second Council Nicaea (787 C.E.), it was decreed that churches should have altars with relics of saints placed within them. The Second Vatican Council (1962-1965) encouraged this perennial practice. In 2010, the *General Instruction of the Roman Missal* stated, "The practice of placing relics of Saints, even those not Martyrs, under the altar to be dedicated is fittingly retained. Care should be taken, however, to ensure the authenticity of such relics" (302).

In his book, *Liturgical Altar*, Geoffrey Webb notes that Church has given artists and architects wide latitude about designing Church buildings. When it comes to designing altars, the directions of the Church are all embracing and exact:

Not only does she consider it the central focus of the whole liturgy, the raison d'être of the building in which it stands; not only does she indicate that the church exists for the altar, rather than the altar for the church; not only does she look upon it as the sacrificial stone, upon which Christ, our priest and Victim, offers Himself daily in His Eucharistic Sacrifice, which is the central act of her liturgy; but she has proclaimed again and again that in her mind the altar represents her Lord Himself. He is Altar, Victim, and Priest.

The understanding of the altar and what it signifies in the Catholic Church reminds us of the need to treat it with reverence and love that is due to Christ himself. The book of Leviticus says, "You shall keep My Sabbaths and revere My sanctuary; I am the Lord" (Lev 19:30). It is interesting because at that time, the sanctuary was a tent, not the Temple, which came later. The presence of the Lord and the mystery that is celebrated makes even the most common setting sacred in the eyes of the Lord. Reverence for things of God carries with it a sense of worship and it involves living and acting in such a way that brings glory to God. The altar is always covered with an altar cloth.

Sacred Linen

Four pieces of linen are associated with the altar and celebration of the Mass: corporal, pall, purificator, and finger towels.

• The Blessed Sacrament and the Ciborium containing it are always placed on a corporal. This is a square piece of cloth that is placed flat, over the altar cloth, during the preparation of the gifts. The sacred vessels are placed on the corporal.

• The pall is a stiff, square white cloth placed over the paten, which covers the chalice.

• The purificator is pure white linen used for cleansing the chalice. It is usually twelve to eighteen inches long, and nine or ten inches wide. It folds in three layers so that, when placed on the chalice beneath the paten, its width is about three inches. A small cross may be stitched in it at its center to distinguish it from the smaller finger towels.

• Finger towels can be made up of any material, preferably linen. It is used for washing the hands of the priest during the preparation of the gifts. Since these linens are set aside for use in the divine worship, they take on a sacred character both by the blessing they receive and the sacred function they fulfill.

Altar linens used in the course of the Eucharistic celebration should be treated with respect and care. In cleaning these linens, liturgical norms should be followed strictly. Because of their function, purificators and corporals regularly become stained with the Precious Blood and they contain particles of the Sacred Host. It is, therefore, essential that they should first be cleansed in a sacrarium located in the sacristy of the Church and only afterwards washed with laundry soaps in the customary manner. Ordinary sinks drain into the sewer system. The sacrarium or basin, drains directly into the earth, thus displaying reverence for what is holy and sacred. Any remaining particles of the sacred species—the Body and Blood of Christ—go into the earth.

Purificators should be ironed in such a way that they may be easily used for the wiping of the lip of the chalice. Corporals should be ironed in such a way that their distinctive manner of folding helps to contain whatever small particles of the consecrated host may remain at the conclusion of the Eucharistic celebration. Similarly, when the altar linen which show signs of wear, permanent staining or can no longer be used should be disposed of either by burying or burning (USCCB's Committee on the Liturgy).

Sacred Vessels

The sacred vessels used in the Eucharistic celebration are chalice, paten, ciborium, cruets, and Decanter (or flagon).

• The word chalice comes from the Latin word *calix*, meaning cup. The chalice is the cup that holds the Blood of Christ and is held in special honor by the worshiping community [GIRM 327]. All chalices used at a Eucharistic Celebration are to be made of precious metals as a sign of their importance.

• Paten is a saucer-like disk, which holds the bread that becomes the Body of Christ. Like the chalice, the paten is made up of precious metal.

• Ciborium is a vessel used to hold the Hosts used for communion. It is also used to reserve the Blessed Sacrament in the tabernacle.

• The pitcher-like vessel used to hold the wine that will be poured into the chalice during the Eucharistic celebration is called a Decanter or flagon. It is brought to the altar during the presentation of gifts.

• Cruets are a set of bottles or jugs that hold water or wine. These too are carried to the altar during the preparation of gifts.

• The altar servers bring a washbowl with water to the priest during the preparation of gifts, so that the priest can wash his hands before the Eucharistic prayer.

Like the altar linens, these sacred vessels, especially the chalice, paten and ciborium, should be handled with respect and care. The presider purifies them according to liturgical norms, then washes the chalice and ciborium with water. This water is poured into the *sacrarium*. How we treat sacred things expresses our faith in the truth of the Holy Eucharist and fosters openness to the graces God gives in the celebration of the sacrament. It is recommended that those who cleanse these sacred linens or vessels accompany their function with silent prayer.

The following story has been narrated many times. I came across it in a sermon by Deacon Greg Kandra:

Back in the 1970s, when there was a lot of liturgical innovation going on, Dorothy Day invited a young priest to celebrate Mass. at the Catholic Worker. He decided to do something that he thought was relevant and hip. He asked Dorothy if she had a coffee cup he could borrow. She found one in the kitchen and brought it to him. And, he took that cup and used it as the chalice to celebrate Mass.

When it was over, Dorothy picked up the cup, found a small gardening tool, and went to the backyard. She knelt down, dug a hole, kissed the coffee cup, and buried it in the earth. With that simple gesture, Dorothy Day showed that she understood something that so many of us today don't: she knew that Christ was truly present in something as ordinary as a ceramic cup. And that it could never be just a coffee cup again.

This story is recounted as the classic example of Dorothy Day's reverence for the Eucharist and for her adherence to the ritual traditions and regulations of the Church.

Presentation of Bread and Wine
The gifts of bread and wine brought to the altar are then offered to the Lord with an accompanying prayer. The priest elevates the bread slightly and prays: "Blessed are you Lord God of all creation, through your goodness we have this bread to offer,

which earth has given, and human hands have made. It will become for us the bread of life." Taken from the Jewish tradition, this prayer pays tribute to the work of human hands and gratitude for the gift of the earth that produces the gifts being offered. The prayer acknowledges the work that farmers put in to prepare the earth, the methods of growing wheat and grapes, and the entire process that gives us bread and wine. These skills come from the Lord and we offer them back to God in the Eucharist. The prayer links Eucharist with the earth, which should motivate us to do all we can to preserve the fruitfulness of the earth. Eucharistic spirituality leads to greater respect for all of God's creation and motivates us towards greater environmental sensitivity.

Similarly, the priest offers the wine to the Lord. He pours the wine from the flagon into the chalice, adding drops of water into the wine with a prayer: "By the mystery of this water and wine, may we come to share in the divinity of Christ who humbled himself to share in our humanity." The water symbolizes the human nature of Jesus, which is united in a mysterious way to his divine nature. The water may also symbolize the assembly of believers, who ardently desire to be united with Jesus both in his humanity and in his divinity. In the 3rd Century, St. Cyprian wrote on this theme what has become an accepted explanation:

For because Christ bore us all, in that He also bore our sins, we see that in the water is understood the people, but in the wine is showed the blood of Christ. But when the water is mingled in the cup with wine, the people [are] made one with Christ, and the assembly of believers is associated and conjoined with Him on whom it believes; which association and conjunction of water and wine is so mingled in the Lord's cup, that that mixture cannot any more be separated.

The prayer for both the bread and the wine mentions the words, "It will become for us the bread of life" . . . "It will become our spiritual drink." These expressions imply the transformation of these gifts into the Body and Blood of our Lord Jesus Christ. They are now set apart. In union with the mystery, it is important that we offer ourselves with the bread and wine, so that we too we will be transformed fully along with His Body and Blood into his image and likeness; that the power of the Holy Spirit which transforms these gifts will also accept our weaknesses and imperfections, perfecting them though the Eucharistic mystery.

Washing of Hands and Offertory Prayer

During the offertory, the congregation makes an offering to the Church for her sustenance and that of the ministers. In ancient times, some brought money, while many others brought the fruits of their labor—cattle and sheep, chickens and eggs, bread and cheese, and lots of other material stuff. This brought about the washing of the hands of the Celebrant, which became soiled from handling these offerings. Today, the assembly contributes only money and the celebrants do not touch these offerings, except in some cases, receiving the basket that gathers the collections into one. Even so, the washing ritual has not been expunged, but rather given a new meaning through the prayer that is silently uttered by the priest.

The *General Instruction* states that this rite is an expression of the priest's desire for interior purification. He turns his mind from worldly goods (money) to things that are God's. The priest's prayer during the washing is about his interior dimension—the desire to be cleansed from sin and freed from iniquity. Thus, using a simple ceremony, the priest transforms something we do many times daily and take for granted into something deeply spiritual and penitential, preparing himself for the Holy Mystery he is about to make present for the community.

The celebrant then invites the community to pray with the words, "Pray, brethren, that my sacrifice and yours may be acceptable to God, the almighty Father." The expression, "my sacrifice and yours," can lead someone to a flawed understanding of who is offering the sacrifice; that the congregation itself is offering the sacrifice along with the priest. That is not the case. The sacrifice, of course, is Christ's sacrifice. It is Christ who offers his Body and pours out his Blood for us. It is Christ who sets the table, prepares the altar and bids us come. Christ is both victim and priest. It is the priest, who because of his ordination is designated and chosen to act *in persona Christi*, thus offering the sacrifice. Priest is the instrument through whom Christ acts in every sacrament. The expression serves to remind everyone that the priest offers the sacrifice on behalf of the Church; that the assembly offers themselves along with the bread and wine to be transformed into the image and likeness of God: "Therefore I urge you, brethren, by the mercies of God, to present your bodies a living and holy sacrifice, acceptable to God, which is your spiritual service of worship" (Rom 12:21).

The offertory concludes with a prayer the celebrant utters over the gifts, thus bringing together into one prayer all the actions, signs and gestures, and lifting the offerings unto the Lord for his mysterious action over them. These prayers often focus on perfecting the inner disposition of the people with awakening words, such as, "Help us grow in holiness" or "Purify us in mind and heart and make us eager to serve you." The assembly responds to the prayer in the affirmative, "Amen." The offertory prayers express a sentiment of gratitude as it acknowledges all the gifts we have been freely given by God; hence, our offering of gifts becomes a "holy exchange of gifts."

Conversi ad Dominum (Turn now toward the Lord)

In the early Church, after the homily the priest would cry out to the congregation these words, "*Conversi ad Dominum.*" "This meant, in the first place, that they would turn toward the East, toward the rising sun, the sign of Christ returning, whom we go to meet when we celebrate the Eucharist. Where this was not possible, for some reason, they would at least turn towards the image of Christ in the apse, or towards the Cross, to orient themselves inwardly toward the Lord" (Office of the Liturgical celebrations of the Supreme Pontiff).

Pope Benedict interpreted this as an interior event, "conversion, the turning of our soul toward Jesus Christ and thus toward the living God, toward the true light." The preparation of the gifts with its prayers, gestures and offerings invite the people of God to orient themselves from within towards the Eucharistic mystery. Despite the chaos that is going on inside and around me—busy, distracted and anxious—it is a call to still the heart, quiet the mind, thereby capturing the glory of the Lord, as he appears in the mystery of the breaking of the bread. That is not hard if we do some spiritual strategizing before leaving home.

Eucharist is a meal that we share with one another. Let us take an analogy from life. You have heard the old-fashioned saying, "The way to a man's heart is through his belly." Well, it seems as if Jesus comes to our hearts through a banquet.

Imagine yourself preparing a sumptuous dinner for a romantic evening with your fiancé. You are excited about it. It is not a burden, but a gesture of love. What would he prefer? Would he prefer steak or salmon? Would he prefer something simple like a sandwich or spaghetti? Why not call his mother to get a few suggestions, or even the exact recipes she uses? If you can learn to cook like his mom, he will love you forever. And then you set the table with his favorite colors, light the candles, aerate his favorite wine and play some romantic music. What you are doing is to turn the meal into an experience—one that is unforgettable. You dedicate an entire evening to love and sharing, and for this you bring out what is best in yourself.

That is what you do in preparing for the Eucharist. You bring forth the best gifts that you can think of, gifts truly representative of who you are. You set the table, say the right words, and bring your best to the occasion. Why? This is not merely a meal. It is an experience in which you feel loved and nourished.

Mother Teresa believed so much in the power of this experience that she mandated her nuns to spend two hours daily before the Blessed Sacrament, in addition to partaking in the Mass, before venturing into their work of caring for the poor, the sick, the unloved and the abandoned. She said that from the Eucharistic celebration and the time spent in adoring Jesus in the Blessed Sacrament, "our love for Jesus became more intimate, our love for each other more understanding, our love for the poor more compassionate."

After my ordination to the priesthood, I was assigned to a technical school in the foothills of the Himalayas. We were nearly twenty Salesian priests and brothers, who managed various departments of technology or took care of nearly two hundred boys in the hostel. Our chef was a grumpy old man, who did not put much love into his preparation of meals. Day after day, we were served burnt offerings. Even God detested burnt offerings in the Old Testament. In one of our meetings, the house members complained about the poor quality of food and the need to hire someone who loved his job and knew what he was doing. Our administrator conveyed the message to the chef, telling him that he was fired. He understood. But he had one request. "Would you give me a recommendation letter?" Now, how do you give a recommendation to someone you have fired for dereliction of duty?

As the community argued over the recommendation issue, Fr. Bachiarello, a retired Italian priest and one of our confessors volunteered to write a recommendation that we would all be pleased with. He wrote, "Our chef, John has left to the satisfaction of all of us." He had succinctly expressed our sentiment.

Do you feel tired of the Eucharistic meal? Are you feeling loved and nourished at the Table of the Lord? As you sit in Church, do you feel your offering is acceptable in God's eyes? Have you put your heart and soul into this feast of the Lamb? It has to do with how you prepare for this meal.

The questions all of us need to ask and answer are: Do I come to this meal with lots of love in my heart for the Lord and my community? Am I in church to fulfill an obligation? Or do I find in the celebration a wonderful opportunity to meet God in a tangible manner? How do I prepare for the offertory? Does the Lord find pleasure in my offering? Am I sincere and fair in my tithing?

These questions have implications not only in terms of our responsibility unto the Lord, but also in revealing an attitude of how important "the exchange of gifts" that takes place in the preparation of gifts really is to us. We give back to God from what God has freely given us. If this "exchange of gifts" comes from a sincere heart, then the giver returns justified by the Lord with a special bond of affection and love, and the Lord will take pleasure in the offering.

From this perspective of stewardship—how much one will contribute to the collection—is a decision we make even before leaving home, and therefore we do not fret or scratch our heads while the Sacred Liturgy is in motion. It flows with the movement of the preparation and is in no way an interruption or distraction. Rather, it is a symbol of the sacrificial relationship with God and an inner union of the self with the offering made by the priest on our behalf. In the spirit of the Liturgy, we can sing or give praise to the Lord together with the worshipping community.

There is a humorous story of two men marooned on a tiny island:

> One man paced back and forth worried and dreadfully frightened, while the other man sat back whistling and sunning himself. The first man said, "Aren't you afraid we're going to die here?"
>
> "Nope," said the other.
>
> "How can you be so sure?" the first man asked.
>
> "Well, you see," said the second man, "I make $100,000 a month and I tithe faithfully to my church. My Pastor will find me."

Many Pastors do not like to preach about stewardship for many reasons. The primary reason is a negative perception among their congregation that stewardship is all about budget or a building program. In the context of the Eucharistic celebration, it is not about budget, but it is about the exchange of gifts. I give back to God generously from what He has bestowed on me. The community does have a right to know and understand how the

Church is utilizing their offering. That is why it is mandatory for a parish to have a finance committee, whose ministry it is to assist the parish administrator in being a good steward.

Preface Dialogue and Sanctus

The Eucharistic Prayers form the center and high point of the Mass. Here we enter into the timeless mystery of the total offering of Jesus. We remember his death and enter into Jerusalem where the drama takes place. The Eucharistic Prayer begins with the Preface, which is like an overture that anticipates the theme of the prayer and provides necessary background information. The preface dialogue is a back and forth between the celebrant and the assembly.

The priest: The Lord be with you.
All: And with your spirit.
The priest: Lift up your hearts.
All: We lift them up to the Lord.
The priest: Let us give thanks to the Lord our God.
All: It is right and just.

The words used in this dialogue give us a clue to the nature of the prayer and gestures that shape the Eucharistic Prayer. The dialogue, "Lift up your hearts," "We lift them up to the Lord," and "It is right to give him thanks and praise," underscore the overriding sentiment and character of the Eucharistic prayer as one of praise, thanksgiving, honor and glory for what God has done for his people. This sentiment of praise and thanksgiving carries into the main body of the Preface: "Father, it is our duty and our salvation, always and everywhere to give you thanks through your beloved Son Jesus Christ (Preface, Eucharistic Prayer II).

Creation and salvation are the two words or themes that make up the reason for the act of thanksgiving: "He is the Word through whom you made the universe, the Savior you sent to redeem us. By the power of the Holy Spirit he took flesh and was born of the Virgin Mary" (Eucharistic Prayer II), or "For our sake he opened his arms on the cross; he put an end to death and revealed the resurrection. In this he fulfilled your will and won for you a holy people."

The Preface closes with the congregation singing the "Sanctus" or "Holy, Holy, Holy." It links the Eucharistic Prayer of the Church on earth with the worship of the heavenly hosts, "And so we join the angels and the saints in proclaiming your glory as we say or sing." The "Sanctus" proclaims Jesus' solemn entry into Jerusalem. Like the crowds that accompanied Jesus as he solemnly and deliberately entered Jerusalem, staking His claim as the Messiah, the assembly gathers in prayer acclaiming Jesus as the Messiah, "Hosanna in the Highest. Blessed is he who comes in the name of the Lord."

On the next day, the large crowd who had come to the feast, when they heard that Jesus was coming to Jerusalem, took the branches of the palm trees and went out to meet Him, and *began* to shout, "Hosanna! Blessed is He who comes in the name of the Lord, even the King of Israel. Jesus, finding a young donkey, sat on it; as it is written, "Fear not, daughter of Zion; behold, your King is coming, seated on a donkey's colt." These things His disciples did not understand at the first; but when Jesus was glorified, then they remembered that these things were written of Him, and that they had done these things to Him. (John 12: 12-16)

In words and songs reminiscent of the solemn entry of Jesus into Jerusalem, the assembly now addresses itself to the journey of the Savior towards his voluntary surrender into the hands of men—his passion, trials, journey carrying the cross, and ultimate death. It is paramount that we set our minds and hearts on Jerusalem at this moment in the Liturgy.

Theology of Time and the Eucharist

A man asks God, "How long is a million years to you?"
God answers, "To me, it's about a minute."
"God, how much is a million dollars to you?" asks the man.

"It's a penny, my dear," God replies.

The man tries to trick God. "May I have a penny?"

"Wait a minute," God replies with a smile on His face.

The story sheds a light on the concept of time for God. God transcends time but acts within it. We humans are temporal creatures with finite lifespans. Space limits us. We cannot be at two places at the same time. God is omnipresent—not limited by space. We are limited by and exist in time. We have a past, a present and a future. We have lived through a past, which was different from where we are now. We know there is a future out there, but we don't know what it entails.

In his essay, "Leading with the Past, Present and Future in Balance," George Ambler said: "We exist and live in the present. But we have a history—a personal past—that influences how we see the world. As people, we hold tightly to the habits and beliefs of our past." Albert Einstein expressed the limitations confronting man on many fronts including time and space, but he talks about the possibilities that exist in humans for greater con-nectedness:

A human being is a part of the whole called by us universe, a part limited in time and space. He experiences himself, his thoughts and feeling as something separated from the rest, a kind of optical delusion of his consciousness. This delusion is a kind of prison for us, restricting us to our personal desires and to affection for a few persons nearest to us. Our task must be to free ourselves from this prison by widening our circle of compassion to embrace all living creatures and the whole of nature in its beauty.

How often we wish we had more time to accomplish the things we love to do. We feel the pressures of life because the pressures of time confine us. Either time is not on our side, or it just keeps slipping into the future.

Space and time do not limit God. He is present everywhere at the same time. He is eternal— preexisting and endless. Due to our temporal limitations, it is hard for us to visualize a state outside time. We cannot conceive of something that has no beginning. God exists eternally outside the confines of time. In his article titled, "A brief theology of time," Paul Mills stated, "Yet within the restrictions of language, the biblical writers convey that God exists eternally. In particular, God's name—I AM WHO I AM—seems to indicate his continuous present existence (Exodus 3:14).

Christ is the 'Alpha and Omega . . . who is, and who was, and who is to come' (Revelation 1:8). The Lord is 'from everlasting to everlasting' (Psalm 90:2)."

According to Mills, God initiated the passage of time in the act of creating the universe: "Hence, time as we experience it does not automatically exist but, as with all creation, was dependent on God's creative fiat for its commencement." What was God doing before He created all things? Augustine responds to this question that *nothing* just like *doing* implies time. Time came to be with God's act of creation, for God is timeless and immutable (changeless) unlike creation, which is temporal and mutable (changing).

God acts in time to bring about his purposes. The story of our salvation is an act of God in history to lead humanity, fallen through sin and disobedience from its original state, back to God. Thus, "God so loved the world, that He gave His only begotten Son, that whoever believes in Him shall not perish, but have eternal life. For God did not sent the Son into the world to judge the world, but that the world might be saved through Him" (John 3: 16–17).

St. Paul paraphrased God's redeeming act in history, "In the fullness of time, God sent forth His Son, born of a woman, born under the law, that He might redeem those who were under the law" (Gal. 4:4). The incarnation is a clear example of God acting in time, "When the time had fully come, God sent his Son, born of a woman" (Galatians 4: 4-5) and in the Crucifixion: a "testimony given in its proper time" (1 Timothy 2:6). Thus, the one and ultimate sacrifice of Jesus took place though the intervention of God in time.

This concept is difficult to comprehend. The fact that eternity entered into direct contact with temporal reality of history, that it exists as "a moment in time," creates a contradiction between existence and the eternal. According to Soren Kierkegaard, the fact that God's presence in time, his sacrificial offering on the cross in time as "a moment in time," can be looked upon as a supreme mystery of our faith, which we cannot comprehend or understand or explain by a function of the human brain. But that is what it took for God, the eternal being to enter into human history and be contained by our temporal reality. As St. Paul put it, "he emptied himself," or in our modern parlance, as Elizabeth Elliott wrote, "he downsized himself to become flesh."

During Christmas, we grapple with the reality of God entering into our history—the incarnation— as a moment in time. In the Eucharistic celebration, we celebrate 'His moment in time' and the redemption that comes from that moment here and now. God is eternal, and everything is present to him all at once. He has no past or future. The sacrifice offered by his only begotten Son is present to him now as always.

Does Jesus die every time we celebrate the Eucharist? Does he pay the price of ransom every time the priest memorializes the sacrifice of Calvary? No. He died once and for all, "For the death that He died, He died to sin once for all" (Romans 6:10). So, how do we unite ourselves with the sacrifice of Jesus? In the Eucharistic Prayer, Christ through the action and prayer of the priest, by the power of the Holy Spirit, lifts us up to God's eternal presence, where everything is present to him all at once. To the community, transported to His eternal presence thorough this act, the one and ultimate sacrifice of Jesus becomes present here and now. Thus, we say the sacrifice of Jesus is made present to us in the Eucharist.

Through the power of the Holy Spirit or overshadowed by the power of the Most High (as Mary was told in the annunciation), in the Eucharistic experience we share in the saving action of Jesus—his action in history, an action with eternal and temporal dimensions. While words and theological concepts help us fathom this, they do not exhaust the mystery. There will always be more to understand. As Mary grappled with the mystery, we too struggle but respond in faith, "Behold the handmaid of the Lord. Be it done to me according to your Word."

Like the two disciples on the evening of their journey to Emmaus, gathering with the stranger while breaking bread and recognizing the Risen Lord, this mystery hard to fathom but possible. It truly happens every time we gather around the Table of the Lord.

Thus, we share in the one and ultimate sacrifice of Jesus, bestowed upon us in the Eucharistic through the power of the Holy Spirit. The fruit of that sacrifice is the gift of his Body and Blood given to us in communion. He broke his body for us. He shed his blood for us. This brings us to an important aspect in the celebration of the Eucharist. The priest does not fabricate the Body and Blood of Jesus in the Eucharist. The one ultimate sacrifice of Jesus *becomes present to us*; we *unite ourselves with His sacrifice*. It is crucial that we allow ourselves to be lifted up to His eternal presence through our prayer and attentiveness. We are redeemed by his sacrifice. Communion is the fruit of the sacrifice. Jesus has broken His Body for us. Jesus has shed His Blood for us.

The Eucharistic Prayer

The Eucharistic Prayer is the heart of the Liturgy of the Eucharist. The priest acts *in persona Christi*, meaning it is Christ himself who offers these prayers to the Father as it was at the moment of his passion, death and resurrection. Together with the priest, all the baptized, who are part of Christ's Body, the Church, offer the prayers as well. The priest offers the Eucharistic Prayer in the first-person plural, for example, "Therefore, O Lord, **we** humbly implore you. . . ." "We" signifies that all the baptized present at the Eucharistic celebration make the sacrificial offering and pray the Eucharistic Prayer in union with Christ.

What is most important is that we do not offer Christ alone. We offer ourselves, our lives, our individual efforts to grow more like Christ, and our efforts as a community of believers to spread God's Word and serve God's people, to the Father in union with Christ through the hands of the priest. Most wonderful of all, although *our* offering is imperfect, it becomes perfect praise and thanksgiving to the Father, joined with the offering of Christ (USCCB).

Structure of the Eucharistic Prayer

1. Invocation of the Holy Spirit—First Epiclesis

The word 'epiclesis' is from Greek, which means to call down upon. John H. McKenna in his *Eucharist and Holy Spirit: The Eucharist in 20th Century Theology* explains the concept as an appeal for the Holy Spirit to transform or sanctify the bread and wine, for the benefit of those who partake in them. The Eucharistic Prayer commences with the invocation calling down the Holy Spirit upon the gifts of bread and wine to transform them into the Body and Blood of Jesus Christ.

Ian Bozant explains epiclesis by referring to the action of Elijah in the Old Testament. Elijah called down the fire of the Lord upon his offering to show forth the God of Israel as the true God, when the Israelites had fallen into false worship (1 Kings 18: 1-40). In the same way, "the ordained priest stands between God and people calling down the fire of the Lord—the Holy Spirit—upon the offerings at the sacred altar."

The Holy Spirit is invoked to effect the transubstantiation of the bread and wine. In the Old as well as in the New Testament, God's Spirit was the way His presence was felt among the people of God. The role of the Holy Spirit is defined as life giving, as in the case of Adam fashioned from dust. The Holy Spirit considered as the breath of God gives life to Adam. "Then the Lord God formed man of dust from the ground and breathed into his nostrils the breath of life; and man became a living being" (Gen 2:7).

In the first account of creation, the creative role of the Spirit of God is emphasized. "The earth was formless and void, and darkness was over the surface of the deep, and the Spirit of God was moving over the surface of the waters" (Gen 1: 2-3). The Spirit of God thus disposes the *chaos* to hear the Word of God in obedience. Then God said, "Let there be light; and there was light" (Gen 1: 3).

During the epiclesis before the consecration, before the Word of God is uttered ("This is my Body" and "This is my Blood"), the Holy Spirit prepares the gifts of bread and wine for transformation into the new creation or the new reality of tran-substantiation. The celebrant may lower his voice and slow the pace of the words to lead the people towards this Genesis moment of creative process. In the second Eucharistic Prayer, the priest invokes the Holy Spirit with the words:

> And so, Father, we bring you these gifts. We
> ask you to make them holy by the power of
> your Spirit, that they may become the body
> and blood of your Son, our Lord Jesus Christ,
> at whose command we celebrate this
> Eucharist. (Eucharistic Prayer II)

A second epiclesis occurs *after* the consecration.
In this prayer, we ask the Holy Spirit to unify the
faithful by their participation in this sacrament.
This is clearly mentioned in the third Eucharistic
Prayer:

> Look, we pray, upon the oblation of your
> Church and, recognizing the sacrificial
> Victim by whose death you willed to
> reconcile us to yourself, grant that we, who
> are nourished by the Body and Blood of your
> Son and filled with his Holy Spirit, may
> become one body, one spirit in Christ.

Thus, through the invocation of the Holy Spirit,
the priest prays not only for the sanctification and
transformation of the offerings and the assembly
gathered in prayer, but also summons the Holy
Spirit to deepen the unity of the people of God as
the Mystical Body of Christ. *Gaudium et Spes* states
that the outpouring of the Spirit which, together

with the Word pronounced by the ordained minister, brings about the transubstantiation of the bread and the wine into the Body and Blood of Christ and builds up the Church as his Mystical Body and is extended further in the history of the world, in the evangelization of cultures and in the depths of each person's heart.

2. Institution Narrative

At the core and center of the Eucharistic Prayer is the Institution Narrative, also referred to as the consecration. If the Eucharistic Prayer is the heart of the Mass, the Institution Narrative is the heart of the Eucharistic Prayer. The celebrant invokes the Holy Spirit (Epiclesis). He then takes the bread and holding it slightly raised above the altar, bows slightly and proclaims over the hosts: "Take this, all of you, and eat of it, for this is my Body, which will be given up for you." Then, the priest takes the chalice filled with wine and holding it slightly raised above the altar, proclaims, "Take this, all of you, and drink from it, for this is the chalice of my Blood, the Blood of the New and Eternal covenant, which will be poured out for you and for many, for the forgiveness of sins. Do this in memory of me."

The narrative of the institution of the Eucharist can be found in the Gospels of Matthew, Mark, and Luke, as well as in Paul's First Letter to the Corinthians (Mt 26: 17-29, Mk 14: 12-25, Lk 22: 7-20, 1 Cor 11:23-26). Jesus chose the Passover feast as the time in which he would institute the Eucharist and would undergo his dying and rising.

With the institution of the Eucharist, Jesus gave the Passover its new and definitive meaning. He showed himself to be the High Priest of the New Covenant, offering himself as a perfect sacrifice to the Father. Jesus changed the bread and wine into His Body and Blood, given now as an offering for the salvation of all people.

The *Catholic Encyclopedia* calls it the Church's Magna Charta, "This is my body—this is my blood," whose literal meaning she has uninterruptedly adhered to from the earliest times."

It is but natural and justifiable to expect that, when four different narrators in different countries and at different times relate the words of institution to different circles of readers, the occurrence of an unusual figure of speech, as, for instance, that bread is a sign of Christ's Body, would, somewhere or other, betray itself, either in the difference of word-setting, or in the unequivocal expression of the meaning really intended, or at least in the addition of some such mark as: "He spoke, however, of the sign of His Body." But nowhere do we discover the slightest ground for a figurative interpretation.

This Church's adherence to the real presence of Jesus—the literal understanding of the words of the institution—was upheld for the first ten centuries.

Early Fathers of the Church (Ignatius, Justin, Irenaeus, and Cyprian) characterized by wonderful beauty and clarity attest without the slightest shadow of misunderstanding the faith of the Church. The Real Presence of Christ in the Holy Eucharist has been a doctrine believed and taught unanimously by the Church since the time of Christ. The Catholic "literal" sense was the only sense the early Christians understood.

Transubstantiation

The Greek philosopher Aristotle made a logical distinction between substance and accidents. He defined substance as something that can exist on its own, does not exist in another, and is not said of another, while an accident cannot exist by itself, but exists in another and is said of another. Take the example of the word 'white' (color). The reality of the word can be said of something, for example, "This bread is white." The color white cannot exist on its own, but in something else like bread. This can also be said about taste. The bread tastes sweet.

The reality of taste cannot exist on its own but is said of another. Aristotle considers these categories as accidents. He distinguishes substance, on the other hand, as something that can exist on its own. For instance, this is bread. In this example, the reality of bread, unlike the reality of white, is not said of something else, but of this thing. Substance exists in its own right. Examples are rocks, trees, animals, etc. What an animal is, a dog for example, is basically the same whether it is black or brown, here or there. A cow is a substance since it exists in its own right; it does not exist in something else, the way the accidents of color or taste do.

The theory of transubstantiation states that during the consecration, when the priest pronounces the words of the Institution Narrative, "This is my Body," "This is my Blood," the substances of bread and wine are transformed into the substance of the Body and Blood of our Lord Jesus Christ, while the accidents remain the same. That is to say, beyond the color or the taste of the Sacred Species, there is a substantial change. Only the substance is converted into another, while the accidents remain the same. The bread continues to look white and the wine remains red. The conversion is only substantial. Transubstantiation is one act by the Almighty and not two processes like annihilation and creation. The substance of bread and wine in this single act now departs to make room for the substance of the Body and Blood of Jesus Christ. Lastly, the entire substance of the bread and wine is transformed into the Body and Blood of Jesus Christ:

So the Catholic doctrine of Transubstantiation sets up a mighty bulwark around the dogma of the Real Presence and constitutes in itself a distinct doctrinal article, which is not involved in that of the Real Presence though the doctrine of the Real Presence is necessarily contained in that of Transubstantiation (*Catholic Encyclopedia*).

The Orthodox Church accepts the Eucharist as a Sacrament (using the term "Mystery" instead of "Sacrament"). It also accepts the doctrines of the Real Presence and the sacrificial nature of the Eucharist. However, Orthodox theologians do not attempt to explain how the change occurs, preferring to regard it as a divine mystery. The Eucharistic service is commonly known as the Divine Liturgy.

Dr. David J. Dunn wrote, "The Eucharist? We call that Jesus. We believe it is actually the body and blood of Christ in the form of bread and wine, but we do not believe in transubstantiation. That is a Catholic thing. We believe it is a mystery. In other words, It's the Body of Christ. Now stop asking so many stupid questions and open your mouth!" In rare cases when responding to the arguments of Luther and Calvin and some Protestant Churches, the Orthodox Church uses the word, *transubstantiate*, but it has never risen to the level of dogma.

Catholic doctrine of transubstantiation is the one single major difference between Catholics and many Protestant Churches.

1. Luther expounded the **doctrine of Consubstantiation**, meaning that the substance of the bread

coexists with the true Body of Christ. Martin Luther likened this to the idea of a red-hot iron in a fire—united, but not changed. Dr. Bock says: "I like to call it 'the over, under, around and through' view.

Jesus Christ surrounds the elements. He's spiritually present, but he's not in the elements themselves; the elements don't become the body and blood of Christ." This doctrine has no Scriptural basis. If Jesus had meant that His Body coexists in the substance of the bread, he would have said, "This bread contains my Body," or "In this bread is my Body." His words are clear and distinct. "This is my Body."

2. Calvin put forward the **doctrine of Concomitance,** which is accepted mostly by the Presbyterian and reformed Churches. In this doctrine, the bread and wine remain what they are, but on the occasion of the Eucharist and of communion they become a vehicle of the real presence of Christ. The body and the blood of Christ, his humanity and divinity, are united in the act of eating the bread and drinking the wine of the Eucharist. In this case, one can no longer see what difference there is between Christ's promise: "If two or three are gathered in my name, I am in their midst" (Matt. 18:20) and Christ's words at the Supper: "This is my body . . . this is my blood" (Luke 22:19).

3. The third view is called **Evangelical Memorial-ism,** which is the most accepted practice among Evangelicals and Baptists. According to this view, the bread and wine are mere symbols. When Jesus took the bread and said, "This is my body," what He meant was, "This bread *represents* my body." This is also called the *Zwinglian* view after Huldrych Zwingli who developed the doctrine. The Lord's Supper is nothing more than a memorial service to Christ, who himself said, "Do this in remembrance of me." Theologians have often scorned this view as the "real absence" view, in contrast to the other three views that teach the "real presence" of Christ in the Lord's Supper.

4. The Salvation Army and Quakers have **no Eucharist or communion** in their form of worship. They emphasize personal faith and on a spiritual relationship with God, which is not dependent on anything external or ritualistic. According to their scholars, the use of sacraments especially the Eucharist has often become a matter of division and bias among Christians. The position held by the Salvation Army is not an article of faith or doctrine, but simply one of practice. They issued the following statement: "The Salvation Army has never said it is wrong to use sacraments, nor does it deny that other Christians receive grace from God through using them. Rather, the Army believes that it is possible to live a holy life and receive the grace of God without the use of physical sacraments and

that they should not be regarded as an essential part of becoming a Christian."

Blood of the New and Eternal Covenant

This expression, part of the Institution Narrative of the Eucharistic Prayer, was spoken by Jesus during the Last Supper. In the Gospels of Mark and Matthew, Jesus says, "This is my blood of the covenant" (Mark 14:24), which resonates with the institution of the Mosaic covenant in Exodus 24:8. The night before the Israelites departed Egypt, they ate a symbolic and ceremonial meal. It was more than a simple meal; it was a memorial.

Jews have celebrated a ritual remembrance of that night ever since. The Passover night recalls the event when God destroyed all the first-borns of Egypt to liberate the people of God from slavery and bondage. On the first Passover night, all Israelite families were instructed to sacrifice an unblemished lamb and then sprinkle the lamb's blood on the doorposts. They were to eat the lamb's roasted flesh with unleavened bread (Exodus 12: 5-8). When coming to destroy the Egyptian children, the angel of death passed over the houses sprinkled with the blood of the lamb. Thus, the Passover marked their birth as a people of God in the covenant He made with them at Sinai:

Then he (Moses) arose early in the morning and built an altar at the foot of the mountain with twelve pillars for the twelve tribes of

Israel. He sent young men of the sons of
Israel, and they offered burnt offerings and
sacrificed young bulls as peace offerings to
the Lord. Moses took half of the blood and
put it in basins, and the other half of the
blood he sprinkled on the altar. Then he took
the book of the covenant and read it in the
hearing of the people; and they said, "All
that the Lord has spoken we will do, and we
will be obedient!" So, Moses took the blood
and sprinkled it on the people, and said,
"Behold the blood of the covenant, which the
Lord has made with you in accordance with
all these words." (Exodus 24: 4-8)

Each year, the people recalled the sacred night
of their freedom with readings from Scripture
about the first Passover and eating the unblemished
lamb with unleavened bread.

Jesus instituted the new covenant in the context
of the Passover festival. He became the Passover
lamb as he offered himself to the Father as a perfect
sacrifice on our behalf. St. Paul states, "Our paschal
lamb, Christ, has been sacrificed" (1 Corinthians
5:7). Jesus' death on the cross was a Passover from
death to life for himself and for all of us. His blood
saves us from death. In 1 Peter 1: 18-19 we are told,
"You were ransomed . . . not with perishable things
like silver or gold but with the precious blood of
Christ as of a spotless unblemished lamb." Jesus

made it possible for us to break out of the slavery of sin and death.

In biblical thought, a covenant is not a contract or mutual agreement between God and man, but an unsought gift of God to man. Pope Benedict XVI in *New Covenant* wrote, "The covenant then is not a pact built on reciprocity, but rather a gift, a creative act of God's love." By declaring the cup to be "blood of the covenant," Jesus states that his blood, poured out in his death and made truly present in the Eucharist, will reestablish the bond of kinship between God and man. In this New Covenant sealed with His Blood, Jesus restores mankind to God's original intent as a son or daughter with all the benefits and blessings that come from being a co-heir with Jesus.

1. Memorial Acclamation or the Mystery of Faith

Since the 7th Century the expression, *mysterium fidei* (mystery of faith), has appeared united to the consecration formula. At first it was within the formula, but now it is at the end. In the new translation of the Mass, the Church dropped the expression, "Let us proclaim the Mystery of Faith," and made it just, "The Mystery of Faith." A *proclamation* is a statement made <u>about</u> someone— while an *acclamation* is made <u>to</u> someone. In other words, the new acclamations are constructed to be more like prayers, rather than mere statements in which a deeper meaning will be revealed. They express a mystery that ought to be lived daily in our lives. In response, the people shall make one of three revised acclamations.

We proclaim your Death, O Lord, and profess your Resurrection until you come again.
When we eat this Bread and drink this Cup, we proclaim your Death, O Lord, until you come again.
Save us, Savior of the world, for by your Cross and Resurrection you have set us free.

All three of these acclamations mention death and Resurrection. In the third acclamation, the 'Cross' is used referring to Jesus' death. The Mystery of Faith is addressed to Christ and is, technically, the Paschal Mystery. All three are rooted in Scripture. The first two acclamations are from 1 Corinthians 11:26, "For as often as you eat this bread and drink the cup, you proclaim the death of the Lord until he comes." Christ's title in the third acclamation is found in John 4:42, where the woman who met Jesus at the well is told by her fellow Samaritans, "We know that this is truly the savior of the world."

2. Anamnesis

Anamnesis is a prayer of remembrance in which the Church recalls the Lord's passion, resurrection, and ascension into heaven in fulfillment of the command that she received from Christ the Lord through the Apostles. Anamnesis is a Greek word meaning memory, but not the same way that we think about a memory. We look at memory as recalling something that happened in the past. Anamnesis is understood as remembering in such a way that the event of the past is actually made present once again.

Steve Raml states:

Our Anamnesis is our remembering, our making present, God's saving deeds in Christ so that the fullness and power of those deeds of the past—his life, death, resurrection and ascension—take effect in our lives here and now. It is with this understanding that we recall Christ's command, "Do this in memory of me."

3. Intercessory Prayer

One of the characteristic marks of every liturgy is praying constantly for the whole Church. The *General Instruction of the Roman Missal* explains that, through the intercessions, "the Eucharist is celebrated in communion with the entire Church, of heaven as well as of earth, and that the offering is made for her and for all her members, living and dead, who have been called to participate in the redemption and the salvation purchased by Christ's Body and Blood." Some of the expressions of intercessions found in the Eucharistic Prayer are as follows:

Lord, may this sacrifice, which has made our peace with you, advance the peace and salvation of the world.
Strengthen in faith and love your pilgrim Church on earth; . . .
Father, hear the prayers of the family you have gathered here before you. In mercy and love unite all your children wherever they may be.

After asking God to preserve his Church for unity and peace, the Eucharistic Prayer continues in prayer for our shepherds, especially the Pope and the bishops. The intercessory prayer is then directed to the community gathered in celebration. The second segment of the intercessory prayer remembers all those who have died, "Remember also our brothers and sisters who have fallen asleep in the hope of the resurrection, and all who have died in your mercy: welcome them into the light of your face" (Eucharistic Prayer II). "To our departed brothers and sisters, too, and to all who were pleasing to you at their passing from this life, give kind admittance to your kingdom" (Eucharistic Prayer III).

Finally, the Eucharistic prayer seeks the intercession of the saints including our Blessed Mother

Mary, St. Joseph her spouse, and the blessed apostles, who are enjoying the glories of heaven.

We express a desire that in sharing their heavenly inheritance, "We may merit to be coheirs to eternal life" (Eucharistic Prayer II). "We may obtain an inheritance with your elect" (Eucharistic Prayer III).

4. Doxology & Amen

Doxology comes from the Greek word *doxa*, meaning "glory"; therefore, glorification or giving glory to God. The priest takes the chalice and the paten with the Sacred Host and, lifting them up, sings or says, "Through him, with him, in him, in the unity of the Holy Spirit, all glory and honor is yours, almighty Father, for ever and ever." The people participate in the great doxology by singing or responding with the Great Amen.

A text from the Letter of St. Paul to the Romans inspired the final Doxology: "For from Him and through Him and to Him are all things. To Him *be* the glory forever. Amen" (Rom 11:36). This prayer of praise summarizes the entire Eucharistic Prayer. It directs the Eucharistic Prayer to God, praying that all glory and honor be given to God through the One Sacrifice of Christ offered in the Eucharist.

In his book, *What Happens at Mass?* Fr. Jeremy Driscoll, OSB, explains the significance and meaning of the people's response to the Doxology:

To this doxology, to the entire Eucharistic Prayer, the assembly sings, 'Amen!' It is no wonder that this is often called the 'Great' Amen, because, 'This is the biggest Amen of the Mass and so is the biggest Amen in the world.' This Amen contains all the others. In the Mass, from our own place and time, we are spliced into this *eternal Amen*, and we shall sing forever what we are singing now. Amen!

The Communion Rite

The Communion Rite begins with an invitation by the celebrant to pray one of our most familiar prayers, a prayer that Jesus himself taught his disciples—the Our Father. By addressing God as 'Our Father,' we bolster our belief that we are one family with God as our Father. We assert that we are all brothers and sisters, that Jesus is our brother and that our relationship in this communion transcends earthly bonds of love and intimacy. It is rather centered on the fulfillment of God's Will and the presence of his Kingdom—"Thy Kingdom come, and Thy Will be done." Pope Benedict XVI said that heaven becomes present on earth in the places where God's will is done. Gathered together in the sacred enclosure, the people of God have created heaven on earth, and now they are indeed preparing themselves for the heavenly banquet offered by Jesus, His Son.

The petition, "Give us today our daily bread," prepares us for the Eucharist in communion. There can be no true communion here on earth without partaking of the Body and Blood of Jesus Christ: "Unless you eat the flesh of the Son of Man and drink his Blood, you do not have life within you" (John 6: 53). The prayer also expresses our desire for forgiveness and mercy as we prepare for the reception of the Body and Blood of Christ. The prayer underscores the essential connection between receiving divine forgiveness and forgiving others. A condition for receiving God's gracious forgiveness is our willingness to forgive those who have wronged us. God's purpose in forgiving us is that we might be reconciled to him and to one another.

The experience of divine forgiveness enables us to prepare ourselves for communion by banishing from our hearts all bitterness and hatred. The final petition in the Our Father has to do with our sanctification. In John 17: 15-18, Jesus prayed for his disciples, "I do not ask You to take them out of the world, but to keep them from the evil one. They are not of the world, even as I am not of the world. Sanctify them in the truth; Your word is truth."

The presence of Jesus in our lives acts as an antidote to the influence of the evil one. In the prayer that follows the Our Father, the priest continues this petition. He asks for the peace of Christ and protection from all sin and all anxiety "as we wait in joyful hope for the coming of our

Savior, Jesus Christ." The prayer that Jesus gàve us as a model of all prayer prepares us for the Bread of eternal life, which is a 'medicine of immortality" (St. Ignatius of Antioch) and "a great mystery that contains God's new and definitive covenant with humankind in Christ" (John Paul II).

The Rite of Peace

The Rite of Peace follows the Our Father. At the heart of this ritual is a prayer to the Lord Jesus, recalling how when he appeared to his disciples in the Upper Room after the Resurrection his first words to them were, "Peace be with you." The *General Instruction* states, "The Church asks for peace and unity for herself and for the whole human family, and the faithful express to each other their ecclesial communion and mutual charity before communicating in the Sacrament" (82).

Archbishop Thomas Collins wrote that the sign of peace in the Mass is related to a verse in the Gospel of Mathew (5: 23-24): "Therefore if you are presenting your offering at the altar, and there remember that your brother has something against you, leave your offering there before the altar and go; first be reconciled to your brother, and then come and present your offering." The archbishop stated:

Before we receive our blessed Lord himself, we say "Peace be with you" . . . We offer the peace of Christ. And, if somewhere in the church, there's someone who has made me angry, or who has done something that has hurt me, or if I have wronged someone, then I start climbing over the pews to say, "Peace be with *you*." Now, that might be more than is necessary, like going to confession in public. It's sufficient and symbolic enough to turn and say to whoever is nearby, "Peace be with you; peace be with you" . . . Giving the sign of peace could be a very sublime experience of what our Lord is talking in this verse. We turn to the person, and we could be thinking, "I can't stand you. Your personality rubs me the wrong way. Your political views are outrageous. Your taste in clothes is abominable. I would not want to go on a trip with you." But then we say aloud: "The peace of Christ be with you." That's the heart of it all (*Pathway to our Hearts: A Simple Approach to Lectio Divina with the Sermon on the Mount*).

In *Sacramentum Caritatis* Pope Benedict XVI wrote:

By its nature the Eucharist is the sacrament of peace. At Mass this dimension of the Eucharistic mystery finds specific expression in the sign of peace. Certainly this sign has great value (John 14:27).

In our times, fraught with fear and conflict, this gesture has become particularly eloquent, as the Church has become increasingly conscious of her responsibility to pray insistently for the gift of peace and unity for herself and for the whole human family. Certainly there is an irrepressible desire for peace present in every heart.

Thus, the Sign of Peace is not merely a symbolic ritual. It is not merely something exterior. It gives flesh and meaning to the petitions expressed in the Our Father we have just recited together. Forgiven by God, we now turn to one another to share the fruits of such an awesome gift. We are at peace with God and with one another. We are at peace with what God has ordained for us in our lives as well as in our world. In exchanging a sign of peace, we reaffirm the truth of the beatitudes, "Blessed are the peace makers, for we will be called Children of God" (Mathew 5:9). With these sentiments, the community surrounds the Table of the Lord as children of one family around the Lord and Savior.

Lamb of God—*Agnus Dei*
In this prayer, the people of God address Jesus as the Lamb of God, an image that draws on the liberation of the people of God from slavery and death known as Passover. We have dwelt on this notion earlier. It is also the title given to Jesus by

John the Baptist, "Behold the Lamb of God who takes away the sins of the world" (John 1:29). The following day, John was standing with two of his disciples. He looked at Jesus and said, "Behold the Lamb of God." He said it a second time. The two disciples heard him, and they followed Jesus, who turned and saw them following. He said to them, "What do you seek?" They said to him, "Rabbi," which means teacher, "Where are you staying?" He said, "Come and see."

As the community prays using the words of John the Baptist, before receiving Jesus in communion, we hear the word addressed by John to his disciples and we follow Jesus. In communion, Jesus himself will address us and invite us to stay with Him.

The Fraction Rite—Christ's Body broken for us

The term, "Fraction Rite," is unfamiliar to many people. When the congregation sings or prays the Lamb of God, the celebrant breaks the large Sacred Host and drops a small fraction into the Chalice. Breaking the Sacred Host symbolizes Christ's body broken for us, so that when we receive Holy Communion we may be one with Christ. St. Paul writes, "Is not the bread which we break a sharing in the body of Christ? Since there is one bread, we who are many are one body; for we all partake of the one bread" (I Corinthians 10:17).

This Rite resonates so powerfully with the experience of the two disciples on the road to Emmaus. "When He had reclined at the table with them, He took the bread and blessed it, and breaking it, He began giving it to them. Then their eyes were opened, and they recognized Him" (John 24: 30–31).

What follows the breaking of the bread is amazing. The two disciples forgot about their fear or the journey or their pain. They left immediately. They were no longer exhausted from Jerusalem to share the Good News. The point here is that the Risen Lord, their strength and courage, was alive. Breaking Bread before communion draws on the symbolism of the Body of Christ broken on the Cross for the sake of humankind. It is the Bread Broken for a New World, transforming our broken lives into the wholeness of the Risen Body of Christ.

Commingling

During the Fraction Rite, the celebrant also breaks a small piece of the Sacred Host and drops it into the Chalice, a gesture indicating of the unity of Christ's Body and Blood. What we receive in communion is the Risen Lord, Jesus alive and well; the Eucharistic encounter is real, personal and intimate. This action is called the commingling. The *General Instruction of the Roman Missal* says this action is to "signify the unity of the Body and Blood of the Lord in the work of salvation, namely, of the Body of Jesus Christ, living and glorious."

Jim McDermott explained the origins of this ritual as a practice in the early centuries of the

Church, when the bishop of Rome would add a small bit of the consecrated host from the prior day's Eucharist to the blood before communion. This was done to represent their belief that what was being celebrated today was not something new but continuous. There was but one ongoing Eucharistic celebration, and each day they participated in it. After that liturgy, hosts consecrated at that Mass were brought to each of the parishes of Rome, and they would drop a small portion into the cup during their fraction rites, symbolizing that their celebration was a part of the bishop's celebration, as well. According to McDermott, the point of the action was to express concretely the unity of all who do or have ever celebrated the Eucharist.

Invitation to Communion

The celebrant holds up the chalice and the Sacred Host and says to the community: "Behold the Lamb of God. Behold him who takes away the sins of the world. Blessed are those called to the supper of the Lamb." These words refer in the Old and New Testaments to the Passover meal in which the lamb is slain for the life of the community; to the words of John the Baptist, who pointed to Jesus as the Lamb of God; to the Book of Revelation that celebrates the wedding feast of the Lamb as a sign of the triumph of God's people. "Behold" carries an implication of contemplation and wonder. "Blessed" connotes God-like the joy associated with the partaker of the Body and Blood of Christ, which no one can take away. It also suggests the supernatural graces received in the sacrament. The expression, "supper of the Lamb," refers to the marriage supper of the Lamb in the Book of Revelation (Revelation 19:7). This is the consummation of all things and connects with the nuptial imagery in Ephesians where St Paul describes the Church as the Bride of Christ. The Eucharist is therefore an eschatological wedding feast at which the whole church, and we as individuals, is joined with Christ the Bridegroom.

The people's response to the invitation to "the supper of the Lamb of the Lamb" is, "Lord, I am not worthy that you should enter under my roof, but only say the word and my soul shall be healed." These words are drawn from the Gospels of Mathew and Luke, where we find the account of a Roman centurion approaching Jesus and pleading with him to heal an ailing servant (Matthew 8:5-13 and Luke 7: 1-10).

When Jesus approaches, the officer remarks that he understands authority and is not worthy (as a Gentile) to have Jesus under his roof (i.e., in his home). He believes that, if Jesus wills it, his servant will recover. The 'roof' imagery has bothered many Catholics who assert that they are persons, not a house.

Valerie Shultz articulated its symbolism well: "If we think of our physical selves, our bodies, as earthen vessels, we do provide a kind of shelter for

the holy every time we receive the Body and Blood
of Christ. Under our roof, we are in communion
with God in a way that nurtures and sustains us,
like a satisfying meal with friends. Even though he
knows I am unworthy of his presence within me,
Jesus enters under my roof anyway."

The expression, "My soul shall be healed," reminds us that that Jesus came to save us. This
reference to "my soul" reminds us that part of us is
eternal. St Augustine said, "My heart is restless
until it rests in God." In Shultz's words, "I realize
that the healing of my broken, imperfect soul is the
reason I come to Mass. If my soul is healed, my
body and mind will follow, even though they may
experience temporal suffering."

The prayer, "I am not worthy," emphasizes
what we know about God and His grace—that we
come to receive the Body and Blood of Christ with
an attitude of humility; that His presence is not
something that we deserve but is a gift given in
grace. It is a gift that breaks down barriers of class
and culture but unites us all in communion of mind
and heart.

Communion Procession and Reception of the Body and Blood of Jesus

USCCB states, "The Church understands the
Communion Procession, in fact every procession in
liturgy, as a sign of the pilgrim Church, the body of
those who believe in Christ, on their way to the

Heavenly Jerusalem." At the invitation of Christ, extended by the celebrant who acts *in persona Christi*, the community approaches the altar together to receive the Body and Blood of Christ.

In the words of the Catholic Bishops Conference of England and Wales, "The Communion procession expresses the humble patience of the poor moving forward to be fed, the alert expectancy of God's people sharing the Paschal meal in readiness for their journey, the joyful confidence of God's people on the march toward the Promised Land." It is through this action of solemnly walking towards the altar that the faithful make their reverence in preparation for communion.

The communion procession is joyous, and its joyous nature is expressed in the Communion Hymn, a prayer of thanksgiving. The *General Instruction of the Roman Missal* describes the purpose of the Communion Chant as articulating "the spiritual union of the communicants by means of the unity of their voices, to show gladness of heart, and to bring out more clearly the 'communitarian' character of the procession to receive the Eucharist."

Liturgical directives about music insist that the Communion procession hymn is not intended to foster a sense of adoration but rather a sense of unity, a sense that we are approaching the Eucharistic table not as isolated individuals but as a united community.

In most dioceses and parishes, the congregation remains standing until all have received Communion, and the priest returns to his seat. The reason for this posture is that the procession is not finished until all have returned to their seats. When the priest has taken his seat, people may sit or kneel for a period of silent prayer.

While I consider this as ideal, it is important to note that the Holy See has directed that the people are free to choose their posture after receiving communion—kneel, sit or stand. The Communion rite is designed to convey a sense that sharing at the Eucharistic table is an anticipation of sharing the eternal banquet in the kingdom of heaven.

Is it wrong to genuflect before I receive the Eucharist?

We don't have altar rails in our parish, but I'm told that genuflecting before I receive the Eucharist is wrong and that I should bow instead. What is the difference? I want to be in line with the rubrics, but genuflecting brings me into the gravity of the Sacrament.

About the posture assumed by the assembly or individuals while receiving communion, I have noticed that some parishioners genuflect as they arrive close to the Sacred Species. On one occasion, I observed someone trip because the person in front suddenly dropped to their knees. I admit I have only admiration for people who express their devotion and reverence in tangible ways, whether it is genuflection or a profound bow. But we need to distinguish between public worship and private devotion.

When we approach the Sacrament as a community, we assume postures that express our sense of unity and shared purpose. We must not forget the underlying principle that the act of receiving communion is a statement of unity. The *General Instruction* is clear and emphatic, stating, that "a common posture, to be observed by all participants, is a sign of the unity of the members of the Christian community gathered for the sacred Liturgy." We should set aside our personal preferences and dislikes for the greater goal of unity and communion among all participants. According to GIRM, "When receiving Holy Communion, the communicant bows his or her head before the Sacrament as a gesture of reverence and receives the Body of the Lord from the minister."

Fr. Joseph D. Creedon brings a good perspective to the challenge faced by many who would like to genuflect, instead of following the norm laid down for proper facilitation and flow: "There is a difference between what is proper behavior at the altar of reservation (tabernacle) and what is proper at the Eucharistic table (altar). Genuflection belongs to the tabernacle; it is prescribed as a reminder lest we forget that the Blessed Sacrament is reserved in the church" (*The Providence Visitor*, Providence, Rhode Island, diocesan newspaper, 1999).

When we receive Communion at Mass, a genuflection as a sign of respect is redundant and disruptive. I can understand the pain of those who truly believe that genuflection or a profound bow is the only way to show reverence for Jesus. My humble counsel is that what you cannot express in an individual posture, carry it with you in an attitude of absolute humility and reverence of the heart.

As the prophet Joel beautifully expressed it, "Rend your heart, not your garments. Now return to the Lord your God, for He is gracious and compassionate. Slow to anger abounding in loving kindness and relenting of evil" (Joel 2:13). Joel is telling us that the grace of repentance is something that God works within the heart. Reverence is not merely an outward change or improvement of one's actions, words, and attitudes, but primarily an inward change of heart towards another. And the God who is gracious and compassionate probes the heart, not just the external display of reverence.

Communion in the hand vs. Communion on the tongue

The consecrated Host may be received either on the tongue or in the hand, at the discretion of each communicant. When Holy Communion is received under both kinds, the sign of reverence (bow) is also made before receiving the Precious Blood (GIRM). The option of receiving communion in the hand has provoked a strong reaction from some who suggest that it signals the decline and fall of Catholicism. Communion in the hand was officially permitted in the United States in 1977, following a special permission (indult) given by the Congregation for Divine Sacraments in 1969.

Today, the US Conference of Catholic Bishops makes it clear that Communion may be received in the hand or on the tongue, a decision that is to be made by the individual receiving Communion, not by the minister distributing it.

Those who advocate Communion in the hand assert its consistency with ancient Christian practice. St. Cyril of Jerusalem encourages communicants to "make your left hand a throne for the right, as for that which is to receive a King." Advocates of Communion on the tongue point to the reverence with which the Body of Christ should be received. This practice underscores the sanctity of Sacred Host and unworthiness of the recipient.

What mode of reception symbolizes the most deferential or the most intimate form of Communion? I would recommend that you follow your heart in making that decision and refrain from judging people who disagree with you. Whether one receives communion in the hand or on the tongue, the emphasis should be on opening your heart fully to Jesus who comes to you in the Eucharist.

What is intinction?

This mode of reception of Holy Communion varies from country to country and diocese to diocese. In India, where I served as a priest for nine years, the priest takes the Consecrated Host and dips it part way into the chalice (intincts it). He then places it on the tongue of the communicant. This practice is known as "intinction." It is up to the local bishop to establish norms for Communion under both species for his own diocese.

Liturgists, especially in the United States, have looked down upon this practice. They oppose it in fear that this practice may lead to a form of self-intinction. According to them, self-intinction should never happen, because the Church tradition has been always that the faithful must receive communion from the priest. Some claim that Communion by intinction is not practiced because it alludes to the betrayal of Judas, the follower of Jesus described in the Gospels as dipping the bread in the wine at the Last Supper.

Another concern about intinction is based on the risk of the soaked Consecrated Host falling apart and dropping to the floor. The normal practice in the United States is to receive the Consecrated wine separately from the minister, who will hold up the chalice in front of you and say, "Blood of Christ." When visiting another country or diocese, it is always best to follow the practice of that Church.

Who can receive Holy Communion?

In the Gospel of John, Jesus said to his disciples:

"Truly, truly, I say to you, unless you eat the flesh of the Son of man and drink his blood, you have no life in you; he who eats my flesh and drinks my blood has eternal life, and I will raise him up at the last day. For my flesh is real food, and my blood is real drink. He who eats my flesh and drinks my blood abides in me, and I in him. As the living Father sent me, and I live because of the Father, so he who eats me will live because of me. This is the bread which came down from heaven, not such as the fathers ate and died; he who eats this bread will live forever" (John 6:53–58).

These words of Jesus underscore the life-giving nature of the Eucharist. He himself comes in communion to abide in us. The Church therefore encourages frequent Communion, even daily if possible, and mandates reception of the Eucharist at least once a year during the Easter season. St Theresa of Avila said: "There is no better help to perfection than frequent Communion." St. John Chrysostom stated that Communion pours into our souls a great inclination to virtue and a promptitude to practice it.

On December 20, 1905, the Congregation of the Council (*Sacra Tridentina Synodus*) established the rules for daily and frequent communion. It stated that frequent and daily communion should be open to all faithful who are in the state of grace, regardless of their rank or condition of life. The Congregation emphasized right intention as a prerequisite in recommending frequent communion, "That he who approaches the Holy Table should do so, not out of routine, or vainglory, or human respect, but for the purpose of pleasing God, or being more closely united with Him by charity and of seeking this Divine remedy for his weaknesses and defects." Furthermore, the Council fathers enjoined two more conditions—freedom from mortal sin and adequate preparation before and suitable thanksgiving after—for the complete and fruitful reception of Holy Communion.

Pope Pius X championed the cause of frequent and daily communion at the beginning of the 20th Century through a series of decrees and clarifications. When Pope Paul VI reduced fasting before communion from food to one hour, the idea was that almost anyone, if not conscious of serious sin, could approach the Holy Table.

One of the noticeable features of the Eucharistic Prayer is unity of the faithful gathered in prayer through the invocation of the Holy Spirit after the consecration. The same Holy Spirit who effects the transubstantiation of the bread and wine into the

Body and Blood of Christ creates the oneness of the people of God as the Mystical Body of Christ.

Reception of the Body and Blood of Christ in Holy Communion, according to the *Catechism of the Catholic Church* (No. 1396), has this effect: "Those who receive the Eucharist are united more closely to Christ. Through it, Christ unites them to all the faithful in one body—the Church. Communion renews, strengthens, and deepens this incorporation into the Church, already achieved by Baptism." Therefore, the reception of Holy Communion truly unites in intimacy and understanding Catholic faithful who share the same faith, doctrinal teachings, traditions, sacraments, and leadership. To receive communion, Catholics must be in full communion with the Church.

Anyone aware of being in a state of mortal sin must first receive absolution in the Sacrament of Penance before the reception of the Holy Eucharist (*Catechism of the Catholic Church*, No. 1415). St. Paul reminded the Corinthian community:

> "For as often as you eat this bread and drink the cup, you proclaim the Lord's death until He comes. Therefore, whoever eats the bread or drinks the cup of the Lord in an unworthy manner, shall be guilty of the body and the blood of the Lord. But a man must examine himself, and in so doing he is to eat of the bread and drink of the cup" (1 Corinthians 11: 26-28).

One of the sad stories of our Catholic practice today is that human respect and conventions have overtaken established norms and the condition of the soul with respect to the Holy Eucharist and its reception. Legitimate reasons preclude a good Catholic from receiving the Body and Blood of Jesus Christ—serious sin that has affected the soul, a lifestyle contrary to the teachings of the Church, and sometimes just not feeling ready and prepared for obvious reasons, for example, a distracted mind (a lack of devotion and attention to the Sacred Mystery) or a heart that reveals a set of attitudes that stand contrary to what communion is about.

Communion among non-Catholic Christians

I have shared this story earlier. As a young priest, I traveled to Switzerland and spent a few days with a non-Catholic family, who were friends of our mission in India. On Sunday morning after having attended a Catholic Mass, they invited me to a non-denominational Church for their Sunday liturgy. I have to admit that the Church was very welcoming and inclusive, for a person of Indian origin in a predominantly white town.

During communion, the entire Church formed a circle along the walls of the Church. They surprised me when the ministers of communion approached me first and gave me bread and wine. And then, they moved around the Church until everyone had the opportunity to partake. It did not matter whether I belonged to that denomination, or for that matter whether I belonged to that Church or the denomination or, for that matter, was a Christian.

That is because they do not believe in transubstantiation. The bread and wine were merely symbols of the body and blood, a sign of fellowship and unity. The question that many people ask is, "Why can't non-Catholics receive communion in the Catholic Church?"

Some people today view the Eucharist as a source of division. To them, the fact that most non-Catholic Christians are not allowed to partake of the Body and Blood of the Lord makes them feel unwelcome and slighted. Mathew Newsome states the Catholic position in a better light:

It is very important to understand that this is not a simple matter of Catholics get to receive the Eucharist, non-Catholics don't. If that were all it was, it would be exclusionary and divisive. But this is not the case, and it is important that the newcomer you bring to Mass, and you yourself, understand this point clearly.

The invitation to the Eucharist is open to all. As St. Paul reminded the Christians of Corinth:

For as often as you eat this bread and drink the cup, you proclaim the Lord's death until

He comes. Therefore, whoever eats the bread or drinks the cup of the Lord in an unworthy manner, shall be guilty of the body and the blood of the Lord. But a man must examine himself, and in so doing he is to eat of the bread and drink of the cup (1 Corinthians 11: 26-28).

The Church wants to remind everyone, including Catholics, that one must be adequately prepared, sufficiently understand, and fully believe the teachings of the Church and the apostles on the Eucharist for worthy reception. You may ask, "If a non-Catholic Christian believes in the real presence of Jesus in the Eucharist and is not aware of any mortal sin, and fulfills the necessary conditions such as fasting for an hour, can that person receive communion?" The answer is still, 'No.' The *Catechism of the Catholic Church* reminds us that the Eucharist completes Christian initiation, i.e., non-Catholics are not in full communion with the Catholic faith, until they submit themselves to Baptism, Penance, and Confirmation in the Catholic Church. It is just and fair to state that full communion with the Catholic Church opens us to communion in the Eucharist.

While Christians share many beliefs, can work together in serving God's Kingdom, and are invited to pray together, many major differences exist between Catholics and others. Some of them include the primacy of the Pope, a Catholic understanding and practice of the priesthood, the nature of the Sacraments especially the Holy Eucharist. Even though the Catholic Church has made progress on the ecumenical front, the differences that divide us still "break the common participation in the Table of the Lord" (*Catechism of the Catholic Church*).

The Orthodox Churches, whose disagreement concerns the primacy of the Pope, Mary's immaculate conception, the *Filioque* and a few other small issues have been, by a decree on Ecumenism, are allowed to participate in communion in the Catholic Church: "These Churches, although separated from us, yet possess true sacraments, above all—by apostolic succession—the priesthood and the Eucharist, whereby they are still joined to us in closest intimacy." The Catholic Church has also stated that if Orthodox Christians ask on their own for other sacraments, such as Penance and Anointing of the Sick, the priests should minister to them (Canon 844, No 3).

The *Decree on Ecumenism* also states that most Protestant Churches "have not preserved the proper reality of the Eucharistic Mystery in its fullness, especially because of the absence of the Sacrament of Holy Orders." This makes it impossible to share communion between Catholic Church and the other churches. As we have established before, Protestant theologians disagree with Catholic theology regarding the Real Presence, transubstantiation, the nature of priesthood, and the sacrifice of the Mass. However, Canon Law makes an exception in emergency situations. Canon 844, No 4, states:

> If the danger of death is present or other grave necessity, in the judgment of the diocesan bishop or the conference of bishops, Catholic ministers may licitly administer these sacraments [Penance, Eucharist, and Anointing of the Sick] to other Christians . . . who cannot approach a minister of their own community and on their own ask for it, provided they manifest the Catholic faith in these sacraments and are properly disposed.

When I arrived in one of our parishes, I discovered that our Ministers of Communion to the sick had been offering communion to a pious Jewish man, who attended Catholic services regularly and asked for communion. The position of the Catholic Church is that we can welcome them to prayer with us, but we cannot extend them an invitation to receive Holy Eucharist. Since they have not received the Sacrament of baptism, the gateway to other sacraments, non-Christians cannot receive communion.

Concluding Rite or the Rite of Sending Forth

After the communion Rite, the priest and the assembly are invited to spend some moments of thanksgiving and prayer. On some occasions, the choir would lead the assembly in a meditation Hymn. In *Sacramentum Caritatis*, Pope Benedict XVI stated, "Furthermore, the precious time of thanks giving after communion should not be neglected: besides the singing of an appropriate hymn, it can also be most helpful to remain recollected in silence."

During the concluding Rites, announcements may be made (if necessary) after the Prayer after Communion. Then the priest blesses the people in the name of the Triune God, during which the faithful make the sign of the cross. The Mass concludes with a dismissal, announced by the priest or a deacon, if present. More than a mere declaration that it is time to leave, it is a call to mission. Pope Benedict summarized the opinion of the Synod Fathers stating that our participation in the Eucharistic liturgy should be translated into a life in imitation of Christ, such that from the Sacred Liturgy springs forth the "missionary nature of the Church."

Eucharistic celebration ends with the sending forth of Christians into the world. As Christ sent his disciples before he ascended into heaven, "Go into the whole world and proclaim the Gospel to every creature" (Mark 16:15), now the same Christ though his priest sends out the faithful to the world to announce the Good News in words and action. For some of us, active participation in the Eucharistic celebration consists of assuming the role of the worshipper in the pew.

In the words of Judith M. Kubicki:

The congregation does not adequately fulfill its responsibility for active participation by simply responding to the prayers or singing the hymns and acclamations. The greater responsibility comes later: it is the response of one's life to the compelling invitation of the Gospel message.

Eucharist is a continuing mystery, for Christ lives on in us. While we actively participate in the breaking of the Bread, God sparks his divine light in our hearts and we become the lamp put on a pedestal or the light on the hilltop for everyone to see. As salt of the earth, we add the flavor of goodness and truth, justice and mercy to everything corrupted by sin and evil. Eucharist is a continuous encounter with Jesus who lives in us and through us. As we navigate through our daily lives and encounters, we transform the world around us and rewrite the worldly culture in the light of the Eucharistic culture—a culture of unconditional love, a culture of blessedness, and a culture of joy.
In the Gospel of St. John (1:17), we read, "Law was given through Moses, grace and truth have come through Jesus Christ."

This is a powerful statement. John later ex-pounds his statement through Jesus' encounter with woman caught in the act of sin. Jesus is seated with his disciples, teaching them. The scribes and Pharisees parade an adulterous woman in front of him. They ask him, "This woman has been caught in the very act of adultery.

As per Mosaic Law the woman should be stoned to death. What say you?" Jesus bent down and started writing on the ground with his finger. He is in deep thought preparing to express his inner sentiments. The scribes and the Pharisees want to condemn the woman citing the Law of Moses, but God in Jesus steps outside the Law and wants to embrace the woman with grace. "Let the one among you without sin be the first to throw the stone." Then, Jesus turns to the one accused and condemned. "Has no one condemned you? Neither do I?" I don't condemn you. I don't judge you. Go, sin no more. Jesus rewrites the law as he symbolically wrote on the ground.

As John said, "Grace and truth have come through Jesus Christ." It is the same grace and truth that is given to us in the Sacrament of the Eucharist. The Eucharistic culture embodies the human and supernatural qualities that Jesus lived and is transmitted through His personal encounters with real people with their real challenges. The Eucharistic culture of undivided love stirs us to go beyond the law and let love and mercy be the core of our encounters with people in the world.

During the year of the family, Pope Francis communicated with the world in his deeply personal, but somewhat controversial document, *Amoris Laetitia* (*The Joy of Love*), which addresses the problem that remarried couples face in fully participating in the Church's liturgy. The archbishop of Dublin recently stated, "There are some in the Church who are unsettled by the ability of the Pope to place himself in the midst of the uncertainties of people's lives." Church leaders and faithful are beginning to comprehend what our Holy Father is asking us to do. The archbishop said, "Marriages begin with a dream. Marriages hit difficult times. Marriages fail. Marriages begin anew.

The Pope stresses the role of the Church in accompanying men and women on the journey of married life and family life, even when the initial dreams begin to fade or indeed fail." The phrase that I love in this document is, "No one should be condemned forever." That indeed is the heart of the mystery of God's unconditional love in the breaking of the Bread.

When Jesus shared the Last Supper with his disciples, he was indeed surrounded by a group he had gathered around Him and yet their hearts were not yet in the right place. The rituals, the words He spoke and then the shared meal—all cast light on how we should conduct ourselves in the real world. In the world of Jesus, there is so much love and service, humility and self-sacrifice, unconditional love and forgiveness, inclusion and outreach. The same values that Jesus lived and preached must permeate our world

What are the characteristic marks of a good and faithful Christian? Is it enough to attend Mass regularly and pray daily? Or, does the Eucharistic celebration prompt us to engage deeply with the world and its challenges? In our next chapter, I will explore the relationship between the Eucharist and Social Justice. We, the Church, profess faith in the One who identified with the poor and down-trodden, the captives and the oppressed (Luke 4:18). Therefore, a Eucharistic culture is one that is lived in the world outside of the Church.

Body of Christ, Broken for the World

"The bread I will give is my flesh, for the life of the world" (John 6:51).

These are words from the lips of the Master as he expounded the meaning of the Eucharist in John chapter six. According to Pope Benedict XVI, "These words also reveal his deep compassion for every man and woman." The Synod Fathers in the *Eucharist on the Source and Summit of the Church's Life and mission* noted that the sacrifice of Christ is a mystery of liberation that constantly and insistently challenges every person of faith. Pope Benedict urged all the faithful to be true promoters of peace and justice: "All who partake of the Eucharist must commit themselves to peacemaking in our world scarred by violence and war, and today in particular, by terrorism, economic corruption and sexual exploitation."

The Synod Fathers made distinction and intimate link between the food of truth and human need. "The food of truth demands that we denounce inhumane situations in which people starve to death because of injustice and exploitation and it gives us renewed strength and courage to work tirelessly in the service of the civilization of love."

Social Justice and Liturgy are intimately connected. Pope Benedict XVI wrote in *Sacramentum Caritatis*:

> Our communities, when they celebrate the Eucharist, must become ever more conscious that the sacrifice of Christ is for all, and that the Eucharist thus compels all who believe in him to become 'bread that is broken' for others, and to work for the building of a more just and fraternal world (#88).

The division between Worship and Justice for the Pope is a misrepresentation of the Gospel. Some of the great saints, Dorothy Day, Mother Teresa, Catherine of Sienna, Thomas Merton, and many others believed fully in the connectedness of liturgy and life and have provided society a model of life that is lived for others rooted in the worship of God in the sacraments.

In her thesis, *Overcoming Division: The relationship between the Eucharist and Social Justice*, Lauren S. Murphy asks two fundamental questions about what it means to be a good Catholic: "Is it one's regular participation in the Church's official worship, the liturgy, accompanied by an intense personal commitment to social justice causes and how one engages in works of charity?" The truth is that neither worship nor social justice is optional. Yet, there is a great divide in our Church today. Two camps—social justice and liturgy—have parted ways to uphold one dimension over the other.

Fr. Walter Burghardt in his essay, *Worship and Justice Reunited,* addressed the rift this way: "In large measure, liturgists and social activists occupy two separate camps, and our Catholic people are tragically unaware that, in the Catholic vision, liturgy and justice belong together and one without the other is not completely Catholic."

Stephen S. Wilbricht, CSC, wrote:

Far from being an escape from the world's anxieties and miseries, the Liturgy is a primary means of experiencing the ways of peace and justice. Liturgy and the pursuit of justice do not put forth competing agendas, for liturgy separated from the world becomes a myopic waiting for a perfect society in heaven, whereas the agenda of justice without a grounding in the liturgy risks forgetting God's role in establishing a Kingdom of right relationship and peace (*Rehearsing God's Just Kingdom,* Pueblo Books).

In this chapter, I would like you to experience Eucharist and Social Justice as two sides of the same coin, both being experiences of the heart.

Social Justice—the most misunderstood expression in today's society

The expression, Social Justice, has become in today's parlance something negative, with socialistic nuances. The two major misconceptions seem to be the distinction between justice and charity and the role of government in justice. The other misconception is equating social justice with socialism, namely, that social justice requires the involvement of government or the redistribution of wealth. "The 'poison pill' that makes Social Justice unpalatable to so many," as someone asserted, "is the apparent need for government coercion." Some others resent what they understand as taking money that they earn and giving it to someone who doesn't want to work.

The *Catechism of the Catholic Church* calls social justice:

Respect for the human person and the rights which flow from human dignity and guarantee it. Society must provide the conditions that allow people to obtain what is their due, according to their nature and vocation.

The truth is neither communism nor Nazism represent social justice as we see it in the Catholic Church. None of these doctrines and their practices came anywhere closer to "respect for the human person and the rights which flow from human dignity and guarantee."

In the opinion of Pope Benedict XVI, *Caritas In Veritate* (Charity in Truth), justice is the principle around which the Church's social doctrine is based. USCCB noted, "Catholic social teaching is based on and inseparable from our understanding of human life and human dignity. Every human being is created in the image of God and redeemed by Jesus Christ, and therefore is invaluable and worthy of respect as a member of the human family. Every person, from the moment of conception to natural death, has inherent dignity and a right to life consistent with that dignity. Human dignity comes from God, not from any human quality or accomplishment."

Does this understanding sound anything like socialism or Nazism, as many people have said? Pope Pius XI introduced Social Justice as a new virtue in his 1931 encyclical, *Quadragesimo Anno*. He called this form of justice "social" because its aim was to improve the common good of a "free and responsible people" by employing social activities closely related to the basic unit of society: the family.

Social Justice is at the heart of the Gospel. As we look at the life and ministry of Jesus, we see Him engaged in social action at every turn. He feeds the hungry. He defends the oppressed. He stands up for women's rights. He loves the outcast, the despised, the rejected, and the sinner, and calls on those blessed in this life to share their blessings with the poor and the helpless. Jesus introduced himself and clearly stated his mission in Luke 4:18-19. He would give sight to the blind, liberty to the captives, and deliverance to the oppressed. Jesus did these things as he moved about among the people of God. Sometimes, Jesus met people's physical needs before He addressed their spiritual needs. At other times He addressed their spiritual needs first.

The Christian life, according to the example He modeled, is clearly marked by social justice. If one is not working towards building God's Kingdom on the earth as it is in heaven, that person is simply not living the Jesus way. Jesus wasn't just preaching a universal salvation message for the world. He was also addressing specific political, social, and racial issues. He was helping those being abused, violated, and oppressed. Involving ourselves within these issues—serving those who need justice—is an example of following Jesus that today's disciples must adhere to.

The Last Supper—precursor to the work of redemption

After the Last Supper, at which Jesus broke bread and shared the cup with his disciples, they left the upper room for the Mount of Olives. While they were eating, Jesus took some bread, and after a blessing, He broke it and gave it to the disciples, and said, "Take, eat; this is My body." And when He had taken a cup and given thanks, He gave it to them, saying, "Drink from it, all of you; for this is My blood of the covenant, which is poured out for many for forgiveness of sins. "But I say to you, I will not drink of this fruit of the vine from now on until that day when I drink it new with you in My Father's kingdom." After singing a hymn, they went out to the Mount of Olives (Mathew 26: 26-30).

The last verse, "After singing a hymn, they went out to the Mount of Olives" tells us that from the institution of the Eucharist, Jesus proceeded to the work of redemption, his ultimate sacrifice on behalf of humanity. In fact, he sings a hymn as he advances to the work of liberating mankind from the bondage of sin and wretchedness. "Jesus sings at the prospect of redemption" (Archbishop Fulton J. Sheen).

Can you imagine the Last Supper without the cross? What would have happened to our understanding of the Eucharist if Jesus had not laid down his life for the salvation of the world? While hanging between heaven and earth on the cross, Jesus looked down at his enemies and those who sneered at him and said, "Father, forgive them for they do not know what they are doing" (Luke 23: 34), even making an excuse for their greatest sin of annihilating the Son of God. The connection between the institution of the Eucharist and its immediate succession of saving events—the passion, the carrying of the cross, showing mercy to the fallen disciples, the crucifixion, the saving words from the cross and his ultimate surrender to the Father—illumines what we celebrate in the Eucharist and its spiritual and social ramifications.

The celebration of the Eucharist (Love of God) without saving deeds (Love of neighbor) degenerates into pious aestheticism. The phrases "which is given for you" and "which is poured out for you" anticipated the ultimate sacrifice that Jesus made on the cross for the salvation of the world. The Last supper concluded with the exhortation, "Do this in memory of me," a directive to celebrate the Lord's Supper as well as to lay down one's life as Christ did for the good of others. Both are necessary and not optional.

The Upper Room, a place where disciples learned to love and share.

Pope Francis celebrated Mass in the Upper Room—the cenacle—in Jerusalem on a Monday afternoon, the final day of a three-day pilgrimage to the Holy Land in May 2014. He preached on the meaning and significance of the Upper Room:

Here, where Jesus shared the Last Supper with the apostles; where, after his resurrection, he appeared in their midst; where the where the Holy Spirit descended with power upon Mary and the disciples. Here the Church was born and was born to go forth. From here she set out, with the broken bread in her hands, the wounds of Christ before her eyes, and the Spirit of love in her heart.

Francis emphasized the lesson of service in his sermon that day: "The Upper Room speaks to us of service, of Jesus giving the disciples an example by washing their feet. Washing one another's feet signifies welcoming, accepting, loving and serving one another. It means serving the poor, the sick and the outcast." The Pope continued highlighting the spirit of love and sharing that prevailed in that room:

The Upper Room reminds us of sharing, fraternity, harmony and peace among ourselves. How much love and goodness has flowed from the Upper Room! How much charity has gone forth from here, like a river from its source, beginning as a stream and then expanding and becoming a great torrent? All the saints drew from this source; and hence the great river of the Church's holiness continues to flow: from the Heart of Christ, from the Eucharist and from the Holy Spirit.

The themes raised by the Holy Father remind us that the Upper Room, the Sacred Enclosure where the sacraments were celebrated including the Eucharist is the place where Christians are transformed into the likeness of Christ, who loved and gave up his life for the world. Augustine depicts Christ saying, "I am your food, but instead of my being changed into you, it is you who will be transformed into me." Avery Dulles states it well, "This transformation means concretely that the ideas, attitudes and sentiments of pastors and faithful are remolded in the likeness of those of Jesus Christ as he gives himself to us in loving obedience to his Father's command. In this way the church becomes Eucharistic."

The transformation effected by the Eucharistic experience impels us to live the mystery we receive in the sacrament of charity. Transformed by the Eucharist we begin to "put on the mind of Christ" (Phil 2: 5) and act toward others with the mindset of Christ, whose vision from the outset were cast in these words:

The Spirit of the Lord is upon me, because he anointed me to preach the Gospel to the poor, he has sent me to proclaim release to the captives, and recovery of sight to the blind, to set free those who are oppressed (Luke 4: 18-19).

Beginning with the transformation of the individual, who now belongs to the Upper Room and shares its culture of love and sacrifice, the Eucharist prepares one for the mission of liberation in the world. "Formed at the school of the Eucharist" (*Sacramentum Caritatis*, #91), we insert ourselves into the world as messengers of hope and a people who proclaim the mystery we have celebrated.

The Upper Room brought together a group of persons who deeply loved and cared for each other. The time for his passion was fast approaching and those whom he loved surrounded Jesus. Although the main ceremony in the Upper Room consisted of a family meal (celebration of the Passover), it was one with strong prophetic overtones: It "was a remembrance of the past, but at the same time a prophetic remembrance, the proclamation of a deliverance yet to come" (Pope Benedict XVI, *Sacramentum Caritatis*, #10).

The celebration of the Eucharist is not merely a family meal of love. It reminds us of deliverance yet to come, a salvific act yet to be accomplished in the world by those who partake of the mystery. In this sense, what we do with our lives in the future, the sacrifices we make on behalf of others and to bring peace and joy—all add to the fruitfulness of the celebration of the Mystery of the Eucharist.

The Upper Room cannot confine the mystery to its four walls, so too our Sacred Enclosures cannot confine the saving effects of the mystery to its confines. Rather, from this source a great river of grace flows into the world of our lives, transforming and redefining what once did not mean anything to us.

Scriptural foundations on Worship and Justice

Sacred Scripture bears witness to the intimate relationship between worship and justice. From the Prophets of old to the writers of the New Testament, there is ample evidence of the unity of worship and social concerns. A number of passages in the Old Testament declare that Israel's failure to practice justice outside their temple or worship space make their offerings offensive to God. Amos cried foul, seeing the injustice in his society and related it to God's rejection of Israel's worship:

> I hate, I reject your festivals,
> Nor do delight in your solemn assemblies.
> Even though you offer up to Me burnt offerings and your grain offerings,
> I will not accept *them*;
> And I will not *even* look at the peace offerings of your fatlings.
> Take away from Me the noise of your songs;
> I will not even listen to the sound of your harps.
> But let justice roll down like waters
> And righteousness like an ever-flowing stream (Amos 5: 21-24).

In the words of Amos, the powerful rituals of burnt offerings and grain offerings are offensive in the sight of the Lord because God stands with the poor, and a society or an individual that does not show compassion to the lowly cannot possibly be worshipping God. Amos exposed the hypocrisy of the community of faith that focused only on worship to the neglect of justice and concern for the poor. Ritual observance and compassion for the helpless must not be separated. What is condemned here is ritualism without the heart. Worship is first and foremost an experience of the heart.

Prophet Isaiah speaks of justice as an act of worship. After the Babylonian exile, he explains why God has not acknowledged the people's worship. According to him authentic worship cannot be reduced to merely external acts of fasting and piety. God seeks justice and fairness towards one's fellow men. The fast, or act of worship, that God requires is that we "loose the bonds of wickedness" and "let the oppressed go free" (58:6). It is to "divide your bread with the hungry and bring the homeless poor into your house, when you see the naked, to cover them" (58:7).

Isaiah says that if you do this "your light shall rise in the darkness and your gloom be like the noonday" (58:10). If God's people would couple their fasting with lives of righteousness and love, then they would see their prayers answered. They would have lives full of light, healing, right-eousness, and glory of the Lord.

Is this not the fast which I choose,
To loosen the bonds of wickedness,
To undo the bands of the yoke,
And to let the oppressed go free and break
every yoke?
Is it not to divide your bread with the hungry
And bring the homeless poor into the house;
When you see the naked, to cover him;
And not to hide yourself from your own
flesh?
Then your light will break out like the dawn,
And your recovery will speedily spring forth;
And your righteousness will go before you;
The glory of the Lord will be your rear
guard.
Then you will call, and the Lord will answer;
You will cry, and He will say, "Here I am."
If you remove the yoke from your midst,
The pointing of the finger and speaking
wickedness (Isaiah 58: 6-8).

Prophet Micah expresses even more lucidly the
teachings of the prophets on the meaning authentic
worship. There are only three acts that God
requires of his people to live a righteous life—do
justice, love kindness, and walk humbly with God
(Micah 6: 8). This is the answer that the prophet has
given to questions raised in verses 6 and 7:

With what shall I come to the Lord and bow
myself before the God on high? Shall I come

to Him with burnt offerings, with yearling calves? Does the Lord take delight in thousands of rams, in ten thousand rivers of oil? Shall I present my firstborn for my rebellious acts, the fruit of my body for the sin of my soul?"

Peter Goodwin Heltzel echoed an interesting perspective on Micah 6:8: "In Micah's challenge he identifies three practices of prophetic ministry: doing justice, loving mercy and walking humbling with our God. In Hebrew poetry this threefold literary device is called a chiasm, where the punch is in the middle. So, for Micah it is merciful love that is the heart of our prophetic vocation." Mercy is the fundamental attribute of God and is the heartbeat of faith.

Pope Francis has championed the message of the prophets in his own personal lifestyle and teachings on the Church's life and worship with his emphasis on the mercy of God and His predilection for the poor: "Mercy is the bridge that connects God and humanity, opening our hearts to the hope of being loved forever."

Joseph P. Gillespie wrote:

Religious rites, no matter how extravagant, can never compensate for a lack of genuine love. External compliance to sacrifice and rigid rules is not as valuable in God's eyes as a humble heart that does justice, loves kindness and walks humbly before the Lord.

As he has stated on many occasions, Francis desires "a Church that is poor and for the poor." In his apostolic exhortation *Evangelii Gaudium*, he grounded this goal in Jesus Christ, "who became poor and was always close to the poor and the outcast."

Pope Francis draws a comparison between the parable of the Good Samaritan and the story of Jesus accompanying the dispirited disciples on the road to Emmaus that ended with the breaking of the bread and the ultimate discovery of the Risen Lord as He is. In *Encountering Christ: Homilies, Letters and Addresses of Cardinal Jorge Borgoglio*, we read:

First, the pain of the wounded man lying semiconscious with no possibility of escape, giving the impression that nothing effective can be done; second, the self-conscious and reason-filled disappointment of Cleophas. In both lies the same lack of hope. And that is precisely what moves the tender mercy of Jesus, who is on the road leading them, who lowers himself, becomes a companion full of tenderness, hidden in those *small gestures of nearness*, where the whole world is made flesh: flesh that approaches and embraces, hands that touch and bandage, that anoint with oil and clean the wounds with wine;

flesh that approaches and accompanies, listening; hands that break bread.

In contrast to the mercy of the Samaritan, the priest and the Levite pass the wounded and dying man in the name of purity of worship. Jesus calls out the inaction of these representatives of worship for their callousness and a lifestyle that promoted separation between worship and the hardships of life. "Go and do likewise," is the concluding expression of the parable of the Good Samaritan, meaning that imitating the action of the merciful Samaritan leads one to eternal life—an act that necessitated sharing of one's resources and time with someone who, in the eyes of the Jewish religion, did not deserve it.

Cardinal Charles Chaput, in his address delivered at the Napa Institute stated:

For Pope Francis, the task of economic justice, the work of incarnating human dignity and solidarity in the structures of our economic and social life is intimately linked to the Eucharist itself. God incarnated himself in a sinful world to redeem it with his love. His Son incarnates himself in our lives at every Liturgy; again, out of love. We now have the task of incarnating that same love in the structures of the world around us through the witness of our lives.

In the New Testament, especially in his Sermon on the Mount, Jesus exemplified the vertical and horizontal dimensions of faith. "Therefore, if you are presenting your offering at the altar, and there remember that your brother has something against you, leave your offering there before the altar and go; first be reconciled to your brother, and then come and present your offering" (Mathew 5: 23-24).

Jesus prioritized human relationships over empty and meaningless worship. In doing so, Jesus upheld the message of the prophets that, while sacrifice can atone for sins in life, sacrifice without consideration for the rest of life, such as justice, fairness and relationships, are vain. Sacrifices are an important aspect of worship in the life of a Christian, but Jesus prioritizes settlement of conflicts, seeking forgiveness, de-escalation of situations and the pursuit of justice and righteousness over the offering of sacrifices.

We cannot choose sacrifice over relationships. In the words of Pope Benedict XVI, the Christians in the early Church "expressed in a dramatic way the unbreakable link between the mystery of the hidden presence of God and the praxis of serving the cause of peace, of Christians being peace." This is beautifully expressed in the song of the angels, "Glory to God in the highest and peace to his people of goodwill." God's glory (the goal of worship) and peace on earth are inseparable.

In his first letter to the Corinthians, St. Paul highlighted the inadequacy of worship among the people of God. In Chapter 11, beginning with verse 17, Paul reminded them that they were approaching the Table of the Lord with a wrong spirit. The cliques and divisions that prevailed among them and their insensitivity to the needs of the poor had rendered the most beautiful feast of love into something abominable in the eyes of the Lord.

But in giving this instruction, I do not praise you, because you come together not for the better but for the worse. For, in the first place, when you come together as a church, I hear that divisions exist among you; and in part I believe it. For there must also be factions among you, so that those who are approved may become evident among you. Therefore, when you meet together, it is not to eat the Lord's Supper, for in your eating each one takes his own supper first; and one is hungry, and another is drunk. What! Do you not have houses in which to eat and drink? Or do you despise the church of God and shame those who have nothing? What shall I say to you? Shall I praise you? In this I will not praise you (1 Cor 11: 17–22).

Paul reminded the people of Corinth that authentic celebration of the Lord's Supper can never be devoid of their kindliness to the poor and other social concerns. The wealthy and the poor

were segregated in terms of where each segment
gathered and ate together during the com-
memoration of the Lord's Supper. The wealthy
gathered in very comfortable and exclusive dining
spaces, while the poor were consigned to the
courtyard.

Priest and scholar George T. Montague described in his commentary on First Corinthians how
this divided and ghettoized celebration diminished
the very meaning of the Eucharist: "The meal had
the appearance not of a banquet but of a series of
picnicking circles or individual dinner groups as in
today's restaurants or cafeterias, separated, however, not by convenience but by class."

In verse 27, Paul stated the severe consequences
of an improper celebration of the Lord's Supper.
"Therefore, whoever eats the bread or drinks the
cup of the Lord in an unworthy manner, shall be
guilty of the body and the blood of the Lord" (1 Cor
11:27).

One can come to the Eucharistic Table unworthily in several ways. It is common for people
to participate in it ritualistically, without participating with their minds and hearts. They can go
through the motions without any emotion and treat
it lightly rather than seriously. Some of us come
with a spirit of bitterness or hatred toward another
believer or come with a sin of which we refuse to
repent. If a believer comes with anything less than
the loftiest thoughts of the Father, Son, and Holy

Spirit, and anything less than total love for his brothers and sisters in Christ, he comes unworthily.

An important aspect Paul's Eucharistic theology is his emphasis on right relationship with God and with others as a basis for valid reception of the Sacrament. In this sense, he summarizes all that the prophets preached and the nuances that Jesus highlighted when he spoke about worship and glorifying God.

Raymond Brown shed a light on St. Paul's understanding of the Lord Supper: "The whole purpose of sacred breaking the bread is koinonia, not division of the community." Koinonia is a favorite term used by St. Paul to identify the union of the faithful with Christ and among themselves. We approach the Eucharist as individuals, but we never really worship alone. Pope John Paul II said, "A truly Eucharistic community cannot be closed upon itself."

In early creeds in the Church, the term applied to the communion of saints, i.e., the believers on earth, the souls in purgatory, and the elect in glory. Joseph V. Corpora, CSC, in "Concelebrating Mass at the Border," *Notre Dame Magazine*, Autumn, 2010, wrote his experience at the Mexican-American border that has touched many of his readers:

> I could not stop staring at the fence with the altar on either side. Here we were gathered as one Body of Christ divided into two. While the Eucharist speaks of our oneness in

Christ, of the One Bread and the One Cup, of
inclusion, the fence speaks of the opposite—
division and separation and exclusion." [The
Mass begins in the usual way with an
entrance procession, but it has to be adjusted
given the wall separating the assembly. On
both sides of the fence cross bearers lead the
procession followed by the image of Our
Lady of Guadalupe, the flags of both
countries and, finally, items people carry
when they try to cross — water, food, shoes
and a backpack. He continues] "I don't know
why, but when I saw the backpack and the
shoes I could not stop crying. The Mass was
bilingual with beautiful music. Someone read
the first reading in Spanish from the Mexico
side of the border. Then someone read in
English from the U.S. side. I was continually
struck by the absurdity of borders. One Body
of Christ divided into two." [A most moving
and pathetic thing happens at the Kiss of
Peace. People on both sides put their fingers
through the chain link fence to touch the
fingers of their sisters and brothers on the
other side. Fr. Corpora did the same,
touching the fingers of another man. He
continues,] "I cannot describe what I experienced at that moment, perhaps the
deepest longing I have ever known for
justice, for peace, for unity, for acceptance.

The words of the prophets, especially Amos, instructed the people of God about a false sense of worship and religion in all its forms. In his letter St. James taught forcefully what God finds acceptable from those who call Christ "Lord." "Pure and undefiled religion in the sight of *our* God and Father is this: to visit orphans and widows in their distress, *and* to keep oneself unstained by the world" (1:27). Our faith and our worship affect every area of our life and determine the way we live daily. It shapes the way one views others, interacts with them, and cares for their needs, most especially for the needs of the poor and suffering.

St. James exhorted his readers to show compassion and to stay pure, unstained by the world. So how are Christians able to practice religion that is "pure and undefiled" and "bring justice to the fatherless"? Does your relationship with Jesus impact others? Do you know when to bridle your tongue for the sake of edifying other believers? Does your relationship manifest itself in a religion of service that helps to provide for widows and orphans so that they will come to know Christ? Does your love for Jesus motivate you to stay away from moral impurity? Raymond Brown stated, "There is nothing theoretical about the religion advocated in James 1:27, a religion manifested in taking care of needy widows and orphans and keeping oneself undefiled by the world." In the early Church, there was a keen awareness that worship and justice go together; that in both the

Eucharistic meal and the care of the community, the presence of the Risen Lord was intimately encountered.

In the primitive Church, the Eucharist was considered simply "agape,' that is "love." Eucharist is the source of charity and celebrates the unconditional charity of Jesus Christ, who laid down his life for the world.

As Pope John Paul II wrote: "Christian life is expressed in the fulfilling of the greatest commandment, that is to say, in the love of God and neighbor, and this love finds its source in the blessed Sacrament, which is commonly called the sacrament of love. The Eucharist signifies this charity, and therefore recalls it, makes it present and at the same time brings it about" (*Dominicae Cenae*, no. 5). When families form around this Eucharistic love, they become, in the words of Pope Francis, "vital cells" for the transformation of the world.

Saints whose thrust towards justice was rooted in the Eucharist

Some of the great saints devoted to social justice and peace rooted themselves in the Eucharist.

Mother Teresa of Calcutta is one of the champions of the downtrodden, the poor and the dying. Elevating the "saint of the gutters" to one of the Catholic Church's highest honors, Pope Francis praised Mother Teresa for her radical dedication to society's outcasts and her courage in shaming world leaders for the "crimes of poverty they themselves created."

Mother Teresa told this story about her work:

One day, in a heap of rubbish, I found a woman who was half dead. Her body had been bitten by rats and by ants. I took her to a hospital, but they had told me that they didn't want her because they couldn't do anything for her. I protested and said that I wouldn't leave unless they hospitalized her. They had a long meeting and finally granted my request. That woman was saved.

Mother Teresa and the Missionaries of Charity established homes all over the world for the dying, the sick, orphaned children, lepers, the aged, the disabled, and AIDS victims. She saw beauty in all of these individuals others had abandoned or rejected and worked tirelessly to save them. The question is where did Mother Teresa find the energy and strength to serve the poorest of the poor?

The answer is simple and clear: Jesus in the Eucharist. She wrote, "Where will you get the joy of loving? In the Eucharist, Holy Communion. Jesus has made Himself the Bread of Life to give us life. Night and day, He is there. If you really want to grow in love, come back to the Eucharist, come back to that adoration."

She explained her devotion and the commitment of her society to the Eucharistic Lord further, "In our congregation, we used to have adoration once a week for one hour, and then in 1973, we decided to have adoration one hour every day. We have so much work to do. Our homes for the sick and dying destitute are full everywhere. And from the time we started having adoration every day, our love for Jesus became more intimate, our love for each other more understanding, our love for the poor more compassionate, and we have double the number of vocations. God has blessed us with many vocations."

St Martin de Porres, was born in 1569 in Lima, Peru, the son of an Afro-American mother and a Spanish nobleman. When admonished by the Dominican brothers for bringing an elderly, dirty beggar off the streets and allowing him to take the saint's own bed while he cared for the sick man, Martin said: "Compassion, my dear Brothers, is preferable to cleanliness. Reflect that with a little soap I can easily clean my bed covers, but even with a torrent of tears I would never wash from my soul the stain that my harshness toward the unfortunate would create."

Where did Martin receive his energy and enthusiasm for serving the poor and the sick? In his prayer life. He had a special devotion to the Blessed Sacrament and to the Passion of Our Lord. Martin lived from the adoration of the Lord present in the Eucharist, spending his nights in vigil, adoring the Eucharist and contemplating the Crucifix, often giving way to ecstasy and elevation. He would then spend the entire day diligently caring for the sick and assisting the socially outcast and despised, with whom he, as a mulatto identified.

St. Catherine of Siena loved the Eucharist and received many mystical graces through the reception of Jesus in communion, which led to visions and ecstasies often lasting three to four hours. Fr. Raymond of Capua told the following story about this holy woman who lived on the strength that came from the Eucharist:

For the seven-year period prior to her death, Saint Catherine of Siena took no food into her body other than the Eucharist. Her fasting did not affect her energy, however. She maintained a very active life during those seven years. As a matter of fact, most of her great accomplishments occurred during that period. Not only did her fasting not cause her to lose energy, but became a source of extraordinary strength, becoming stronger in the afternoon, after having received our Lord in His Eucharist.

In the words of Cynthia Trainque:

It was Catherine's tremendous love of Jesus in the Eucharist that allowed her to go out to the poor and especially the very ill and to minister to them as she did. Wasn't this the

Eucharistic spirituality that Mother Teresa of Calcutta lived out, too—so that she could pick up the dying from the gutters of the slums, carry them to one of her clinics and care for them until they either got better or died with dignity?

As Mother Teresa acknowledged many times in her lifetime that love and devotion to the Eucharist and the Blessed Sacrament gave her and his sisters the energy and compassion to reach out to the poorest of the poor. They took very seriously the words of Jesus in Matthew 25:40: "Whatever you do to the least of my brethren you do unto me."

Fathers of the Church and their words

It is important underscore the teachings of our Fathers of the Church and to add their voices to the chorus of prophets, apostles and saints as they unraveled the intimate connection between Eucharist and justice. The Fathers of the Church have made a significant contribution to the understanding of the Eucharist. Many of the early Fathers of the Church were persecuted and martyred in the footsteps of their Master and Lord. The Eucharist, which celebrates Jesus' own martyrdom and His ultimate sacrifice enabled them to brave the enemies of the Kingdom in their pursuit for holiness.

Bertilla Fracca summarized the teaching of the Fathers in these words: "The Eucharist is the extension of the Incarnation, it is the union with the Trinity, the sacrament of mercy, the sign of unity and the bond of charity." Below are some of the thoughts of the early Fathers.

The food of truth demands that we denounce inhumane situations in which people starve to death because of injustice and exploitation, and it gives us renewed strength and courage to work tirelessly in the service of the civilization of love.
—St. Ignatius of Antioch

Do you wish to honor the Body of Christ? Do not ignore Him when he is naked. Do not pay homage in the temple clad in silk—only then to neglect Him outside where He suffers cold and nakedness. He who said, 'This is my body' is the same One who said, 'You saw Me hungry and you gave Me no food' and 'Whatever you did for the least of My brothers, you did also for Me.' What good is it if the Eucharistic Table is overloaded with golden chalices, when He is dying of hunger? Start by satisfying His hunger, and then, with what is left, you may adorn the altar as well. The temple of our afflicted neighbor's body is more holy than the altar of stone on which you celebrate the holy sacrifice. You are able to contemplate this altar everywhere, in the

street and in the open squares.
—St. John Chrysostom

If you are the body and members of Christ,
then it is your sacrament that is placed on the
table of the Lord; it is your sacrament that
you receive. To that which you are you
respond, 'Amen' ('Yes, it is true!'), and by
responding to it you assent to it. For you hear
the words, 'the Body of Christ,' and respond,
'Amen.' Be then a member of the Body of
Christ that your Amen may be true.
— St. Augustine

Recent Popes on Justice and the Eucharist
Recent Popes in our Church have also
emphasized the direct connection between our
universal celebration of the Eucharist and taking
action to help those in need. The Eucharist changes
bread and wine; it also changes us. It has a
transformative power and potential for personal
and global transformation. Not only does the
Eucharist call us to action, it nourishes us and
strengthens us in virtue, so we can carry out the
Church's mission in the world: the mission of
justice. The following quotes are taken from our
recent Popes.

And a devotion to the Eucharist that is
ardent, constant and that carries over into
works also has the effect of nourishing and

fostering the inner perfection of his soul and assuring him, as he carries out his apostolic duties, of an abundance of the supernatural powers that the strongest workers for Christ must have.
—Pope John XXIII

The Eucharist not only provides the interior strength needed for mission but is also—in some places—*its plan*. For the Eucharist is a mode of being, which passes from Jesus into each Christian, through whose testimony it is meant to spread throughout society and culture.
—Pope John Paul II

Give us this day our daily bread . . . obliges us to do everything possible in cooperation with international, state and private institutions, to end or at least reduce the scandal of hunger and malnutrition. . . . The Christian laity, formed at the school of the Eucharist, are called to assume their specific political and social responsibilities.
—Pope Benedict XVI

The Church urgently needs the deep breath of prayer, and to my great joy groups devoted to prayer and intercession, the prayerful reading of God's word and the perpetual adoration of the Eucharist are

growing at every level of ecclesial life. Even
so, we must reject the temptation to offer a
privatized and individualistic spirituality
which ill accords with the demands of
charity, to say nothing of the implications of
the incarnation. There is always the risk that
some moments of prayer can become an
excuse for not offering one's life in mission; a
privatized lifestyle can lead Christians to
take refuge in some false forms of spirituality.

—Pope Francis

Summary

"Go in peace to love and serve the Lord." We
hear those words at the end of every Mass. We
serve the Lord best by serving the needs of others.
We love the Lord best by showing his love to
others. According to Greg Colley, the Eucharist
awakens us to our own dignity and to that of the
others. "Then he took the bread, said the blessing,
broke it, and gave it to them, saying, "This is my
body, which will be given up for you. . . ."

These words point to the greatest theological
virtue, *caritas*, also known as charity or love. *Caritas*
is the theological backbone of Catholic Social
Teaching. Without love, there is no true justice. In
the Eucharistic encounter with Christ's love for us,
and realizing our own deep needs, we become
sensitized to all who suffer. Their reality becomes a

reality for us. As St. Augustine said, "The pain of one, even the smallest member, is the pain of all." Colley further stated:

Drawn into the dynamic of Christ's self-giving, we are moved to self-giving action in solidarity with all members of the human family who face injustice. In the Eucharistic encounter, we are challenged to recognize and confront the human structures of injustice, including racism, poverty, violence, exploitation, and all other systemic violations of human life and dignity.

And so, we respond to the final exhortation of the Mass, "Go in peace to love and serve the Lord," by living out in our day-to-day lives the example of Jesus who laid down his life for the many. We go forth to fulfill Jesus' command to love those in need (Mathew 25: 34-40) and be counted among the blessed:

Then the King will say to those on His right, "Come, you who are blessed of My Father, inherit the kingdom prepared for you from the foundation of the world. For I was hungry, and you gave Me *something* to eat; I was thirsty, and you gave Me *something* to drink; I was a stranger, and you invited Me in; naked, and you clothed Me; I was sick, and you visited Me; I was in prison, and you came to Me."

Then the righteous will answer Him, "Lord, when did we see You hungry, and feed You, or thirsty, and give You *something* to drink? And when did we see You a stranger, and invite You in, or naked, and clothe You? When did we see You sick, or in prison, and come to You?"

The King will answer and say to them, "Truly, I say to you to the extent that you did it to one of these brothers of Mine, *even* the least *of them*, you did it to Me."

We see in this passage that Christ identifies himself not with those blessed who serve, but with the hungry, the thirsty, the strangers, the naked, the sick, and the prisoners. According to William T. Cavanaugh:

What is most radical about Matthew 25 is not that we will be rewarded for doing good to the downtrodden, but that the downtrodden are in fact Christ. The further implication is that, as we too are assimilated to Christ, the difference between 'us' and 'them,' the difference between those who serve and those who are served, is radically effaced.

In Eucharistic Prayer II, we entreat God to bring us to "the fullness of charity." It is the essence and goal of our worship that we live fully the love that we celebrate in the Eucharist. Let us rise, then and "be on our way" (John 14:31); let us "rise from our slumber" (Rom. 13:11) to do all the good we can to those whom the world despises and who "count for nothing" (1 Cor. 1:27).

In *Sacramentum Caritatis*, Pope Benedict XVI observed that secularization has "relegated the Christian faith to the margins of life as if it were irrelevant to everyday affairs." Caught up in the overriding sway of the secular culture, many Catholics have dropped Sunday worship and substituted it for sports, athletics, or other recreational pursuits. This has prevented many in our culture from experiencing the mystery of God's love in the Eucharist and other sacraments. The truth of the matter is that the Christian community is rooted in the Eucharist. It is Eucharistic culture, not the secular culture, that should prevail in the life of a Christian community which transforms us into a Eucharistic community. While appreciating and incorporating the unique gifts our secular culture has to offer, our mission is to form a 'Eucharistic culture' in the midst of society (Ronald Lewinski and Andrew Liaugminas).

In the words of the Pope Benedict XVI, "The Eucharist becomes a criterion for our evaluation of everything that Christianity encounters in different cultures." It is true that the social justice impli-cations of the Eucharist present a challenge to every Catholic community that shares in this sacrament of Christ's unconditional love. I would like to share

with you a few questions posed by Ronald Lewinski and Andrew Liaugminas in their essay, "The
Eucharist Changes the World: Effects on Society
and Culture."

Questions for Reflection

1. How can the Eucharist help us recover faith from
the margins of life?
2. What are some values in society that are contrary
to the values we find in the Eucharist?
3. How is our participation in the Eucharist a
radical call to imitate Christ's self-emptying love?
4. What in our society awaits to be transformed by
what we celebrate at the altar?
5. What is the hope you see rising from the
Eucharistic mystery?
6. How can we foster, in our Eucharistic communities, a deeper appreciation for the missionary
dimensions of the Eucharist?
7. How would you sum up Pope Benedict XVI's
teaching on the effects of the Eucharist on us as
individuals and as a community of faith in the
world?

Dr. Donald deMarco looks at social justice as a
divine mandate that is sustained with the bread of
life:

It cannot be ignored. But the life for
Christians that animates their social-justice

activities is Christ's own life, for without him we can do nothing (John 15:5). The Christian mandate is clear: First avail yourself of his life, then bring that very life to others. Everything begins and has its vivifying root in Christ. If one is performing acts of social justice, how much more fruitful would these acts be if they were animated by the Bread of Life? We cannot sustain the effect without constantly renewing the cause.

In his apostolic exhortation on the family, *Amoris Laetitia (The Joy of Love)*, Pope Francis makes a connection between the Eucharist and our call to create a more just world. The Pope wrote:

The Eucharist demands that we be members of the one body of the Church. Those who approach the Body and Blood of Christ may not wound that same Body by creating scandalous distinctions and divisions among its members.

He further explains:

When those who receive it turn a blind eye to the poor and suffering, or consent to various forms of division, contempt and inequality, the Eucharist is received unworthily. On the other hand, families who are properly disposed and receive the Eucharist regularly,

reinforce their desire for fraternity, their
social consciousness, and their commitment
to those in need."

Worship Without Words

In her book, *Eat, Pray, Love,* Elizabeth Gilbert shares a story that I have read in the books of Antony De Mello. Her rendition of the fable goes this way:

The Indians around here tell a cautionary fable about a great saint who was always surrounded in his Ashram by loyal devotees. For hours a day, the saint and his followers would meditate on God. The only problem was that the saint had a young cat, an annoying creature, who used to walk through the temple meowing and purring and bothering everyone during meditation. So the saint, in all his practical wisdom, commanded that the cat be tied to a pole outside for a few hours a day, only during meditation, so as to not disturb anyone. This became a habit—tying the cat to the pole and then meditating on God—but as years passed, the habit hardened into religious ritual. Nobody could meditate unless the cat was tied to the pole first. Then one day the

cat died. The saint's followers were panic-
stricken. It was a major religious crisis—how
could they meditate now, without a cat tied
to a pole? How would they reach God? In
their minds, the cat had become the means.

If one is new to liturgical worship or if you are a
"cradle Catholic," you will find yourself
surrounded by images, traditions and a language
(liturgical language) that is often difficult to
understand, but they are powerful expressions of
the divine reality that they symbolize or verbalize.
Rituals can enhance our lives, especially our
relationship to the divine, in a non-magical way.
They provide comfort, they soothe us, and they
calm us and make life taste better.

Religion can sometimes be superstitious as in
the aforementioned story, when they lose their
original meaning and purpose. Some build their
faith on an irrational belief that an object, action, or
circumstance not logically related to a course of
events influences its outcome. Though these actions
and objects may appear to be rituals and symbols,
they are often driven by ignorance of the laws of
God or Science or by faith in magic or chance. In
general, superstitions don't spark deep movements
of love and concern for serious living and doing
good to others.

Eucharist is a Sacrament. In the 5th Century, St.
Augustine described sacrament as an "outward and

visible sign of inward and invisible grace." *Sacrosanctum Concilium* (*The Constitution on the Sacred Liturgy*) tells us, "The purpose of the sacraments is to sanctify, to build up the Body of Christ and, finally, to worship God. Because they are signs, they also instruct. They not only presuppose faith, but by words and objects they also nourish, strengthen, and express it" (59). Therefore, by its very definition as a sacrament, the Eucharist embodies signs and symbols, words and gestures, postures and dispositions that enhance the outpouring of grace and strengthen the unity of the faithful as the Body of Christ.

Language can be used on two levels: the literal, describing things exactly as they are, and the symbolic, expressing a deeper meaning. Symbolic language uses figures of speech such as metaphor, simile, and analogy, or they can embrace certain gestures and postures that lend depth to the words being uttered. Symbolic language is necessary to describe the intangible aspects of human experience: emotions, intuitions, spirituality, and virtues. These experiences open up levels of reality otherwise closed to us.

Just as there are two levels of meaning in language, there are also two levels of meaning operating within reality at all times: the natural and obvious on the one hand, and the deeper, spiritual, and less obvious on the other. Paul Tillich said, "Man's ultimate concern must be expressed symbolically, because symbolic language alone is able to express the ultimate." They unlock dimensions of the soul, which correspond to dimensions of reality unlocked for us.

Karl Rahner points out that a symbol is "that through which a reality expresses itself." He noted that every being in order to become itself must express itself. The expression of the self is the symbol or gesture or a posture. This symbol represents or 'makes' the self. For this reason, there is an intimate connection between the symbol and the reality it expresses. It is not the fullness of the reality, but an expression of the reality that makes it present to itself and to others. Theologically, symbols and symbolic actions have profound meaning that is communicated in a tangible fashion. It is possible for the most mundane and ordinary object to become something profound, because it is associated with a person we love deeply, or a loving act someone performed for us.

The *Catechism of the Catholic Church* acknowledges the importance of signs and symbols, gestures and postures when it states: "In human life, signs and symbols occupy an important place. As a being at once body and spirit, man expresses and perceives spiritual realities through physical signs and symbols. As a social being, man needs signs and symbols to communicate with others, through language, gestures and actions. The same holds true for his relationship with God."

In summary, we can describe signs and symbols as intrinsically related to the reality they express;

symbols are rich in meaning; symbols evoke a response; symbols are concrete; but sometimes symbols are ambiguous. All of these characteristics are used to great advantage in liturgical celebrations.

Judith M. Kubicki in her essay, "More than Words: The many symbols of the Liturgy," observed that because it is ritual activity, liturgy speaks in many other ways than simply through words. These nonverbal ways of communicating are often neglected to the detriment of meaningful liturgical prayer. According to her, the language of the Eucharistic Liturgy is more than words read from a printed Missal or Sacramentary: "The language of the liturgy, itself a symbol, also includes other symbols and symbolic actions. All elements of the liturgy (bread, wine, cup, water, fire, book, vesture, altar, crucifix), all gestures and postures (processing, bowing, eating, drinking, signing, singing, sprinkling, standing, kneeling) and all environmental elements (art and architecture, color and texture, light and darkness, sound and silence) can be said to make up the matrix of symbols that constitute the liturgy."

For this reason, the promotion of full, active and conscious participation in the Liturgy requires more care and attention to the way we celebrate the nonverbal language expressed through signs and symbols. In this chapter, we will explore the meaning and significance of signs, symbols, gestures, and posture used during the celebration of the Mass. These are not merely ceremonial but carry profound meaning and significance when carried out with respect and devotion, care and attention. They enrich the active and conscious participation in the Mass.

In the Gospel of Mathew (15:8), Jesus said, "This people honors me with their lips, but their heart is far from me; in vain do they worship me." Worship is first and foremost an experience of the heart. Words, lips and the heart must be in sync as one prays. When our whole person—body, mind and spirit—engages in prayer, it is easy to pray with greater attentiveness. In his encounter with the woman of Samaria, Jesus describes authentic worship in these terms, "You worship what you do not know; we worship what we know, for salvation is from the Jews. But an hour is coming, and now is, when the true worshipers will worship the Father in spirit and truth; for such people the Father seeks to be His worshipers. God is spirit, and those who worship Him must worship in spirit and truth."

The expression, "We worship what we know," assumes understanding and knowledge of the mysteries that are celebrated. Every gesture, every symbol or posture in the celebration of the Sacraments is made or undertaken with a deep awareness of what they stand for and embodies an attitude that reveals the great mystery of God. The two words, "spirit and truth," correspond to the 'how' and the 'whom' of worship. Worshipping in spirit is the opposite of worshipping in merely external ways. It is the opposite of formalism and traditionalism. Worshipping in truth presumes an adequate understanding and knowledge of who God is. Therefore, authentic worship emerges from the spirit within and is based on true understanding of God.

External signs and gestures mean nothing unless they establish deep and intimate connections between God as He is and worshippers as they are. Signs and gestures engage the whole person, emotions and thought. Jonathan Edwards, a pastor of a church community said, "I should think myself in the way of my duty, to raise the affections of my hearers as high as I possibly can, provided they are affected with nothing but truth, and with affections that are not disagreeable to the nature of what they are affected with." In the encounter with the woman of Samaria, Jesus elevated her affections from things mundane to things deeply spiritual, from inadequate worship that was characterized by ignorance and superstition to recognizing God as He stood before her and finally requesting Him to give her the living water. Through a variety of symbols and gestures, words and revelations, Jesus unravels the meaning of worship and leads her to conversion that comes from an encounter with the real God.

Postures

"And lifting up His eyes to heaven, He said, "Father, the hour has come; glorify Your Son, that the Son may glorify You" (John 17:3).

During Mass, we assume a number of postures: standing, kneeling, and sitting. In the Biblical accounts, we are introduced to a variety of postures. Abraham fell upon his face before God (Genesis 17: 3,17). Moses prayed with his hands outstretched (Exodus 9: 27-29).

The posture of extending hands is reserved to the celebrant during Mass. As a sign of unity within the priesthood, the principal celebrant and concelebrating priests extend their hands together at different times during the Eucharistic Prayer, during the Lord's Prayer, or for a blessing. King Solomon knelt in prayer (1 Kings 8:54). Jesus prayed looking into heaven (Mark 6:41), John 11:41, 17:1).

Praying to God does not require any physical position, but postures give expression to the attitudes of our hearts. Mathew H. Young states that our posture during prayer matters because the physical body reflects or prompts our spiritual or mental state:

Just as a church or synagogue might be adorned differently to reflect different feasts or to commemorate particular blessings, we might adopt different physical tones to underscore the intention or heart of our prayers. To fall on your face in front of a king signified the complete control he had over your life. Lying prostrate before the cross reflects our acknowledgement of God's omnipotence. We hide our face in shame, raise our hands in joy, or bow our heads in contrition. Kneeling for prayer is a tangible confession of Christ's lordship.

Jesus prayed, "lifting His eyes to heaven." When we lift our eyes to the heavens, we proclaim God's glory and speak about the work of His hands (Psalm 19:1), visually embracing the Creator of heaven and earth. Of course, glory is not confined to heaven alone, for He fills both heaven and earth. Different dispositions will dictate different postures for prayer. In the Gospel of Luke, the tax collector hung his head in shame and repentance over his sins, while beating his breast. The prayer of a humble person will reflect the posture of King David, who lay prostrate on the ground while fasting for the welfare of his dying child (2 Samuel 12:16). Jesus changed his posture of prayer in the Garden of Gethsemane by kneeling (Luke 22:41) and even falling on His face in anguish (Matthew 26:29). Let us explore some of the postures assumed in the celebration of the Holy Eucharist.

1. Standing

Standing is a sign of respect and honor. When I was young and lived with my parents, every time that my Father entered the home from outside, we all stood up as a sign of respect and honor. As a priest, one of the most loving things I like to do is to visit our school children in their classrooms, where they will all stand up together and wish me in a chorus the appropriate greeting of the day. We stand during the national anthem or the pledge of allegiance.

In the letter to the Colossians (5:1), standing has been a stance of those who are set free by Christ: "It was for freedom that Christ set us free; therefore, keep standing firm and do not be subject again to a yoke of slavery." When we stand before God, we assume the posture of someone who is redeemed and set free by Christ. We stand when the celebrant and the other ministers process into the church. We stand for the Gospel because we acknowledge it is Christ himself speaking to us when it is proclaimed. The bishops of the United States have chosen standing as the normal posture for the reception of Holy Communion in this country.

2. Kneeling

In the letter to the Philippians 2: 5–11, St. Paul explains to his readers the meaning and the significance of why we should "bend our knee" at the name of Jesus:

Have among yourselves the same attitude that is also yours in Christ Jesus, Who, though he was in the form of God, did not regard equality with God something to be grasped. Rather, he emptied himself, taking the form of a slave, coming in human likeness; and found human in appearance he humbled himself, becoming obedient to death, even death on a cross. Because of this, God greatly exalted him and bestowed on him the name that is above every name, that at the name of Jesus every knee should bend, of those in heaven and on earth and under the earth, and every tongue confess that Jesus Christ is Lord, to the glory of God the Father.

Pope Benedict, before his elevation to the papacy, wrote in *The Spirit of the Liturgy*, "The Christian Liturgy is a cosmic Liturgy precisely because it bends the knee before the crucified and exalted Lord. Here is the center of authentic culture—the culture of truth. The humble gesture by which we fall at the feet of the Lord inserts us into the true path of life of the cosmos." The Pope also stated, "The man who learns to believe learns also to kneel, and a faith or liturgy no longer familiar with kneeling would be sick at the core." Kneeling is not only a Christian gesture, but also a Christological one.

There are many passages in the Old and New Testaments that bear witness to the gesture of

kneeling before God and His presence. In the
Gospel of Mark, a leper falls to his knees before
Jesus saying, "If you will, you can make me clean."
While this is not an act of adoration, it expresses in
bodily form dependence in a power beyond what
he ever knew. The word for kneeling in adoration
in the Gospels is *proskynein* and it has the meaning
of worship. The bodily and spiritual meanings of
this word are inseparable.

Pope Benedict states:

The bodily gesture itself is the bearer of the
spiritual meaning, which is precisely that of
worship. Without the worship, the bodily
gesture would be meaningless, while the
spiritual act must, of its very nature because
of the psychosomatic unity of man, express
itself in the bodily gesture.

The Pope asserts that kneeling as a posture must
be rediscovered in prayer and worship so that, in
our prayer, we remain in fellowship with the
apostles and martyrs, in fellowship with the whole
cosmos, indeed in union with Jesus Christ Himself.

In the Mass, we are invited to kneel during the
Eucharistic Prayer from after the singing of the
Holy, Holy, until after the singing of the Great
Amen. These are sacred moments when we submit
ourselves in adoration and worship before the
crucified Lord and participate in His ultimate
sacrifice of Love for the cosmos.

The Eucharist is a cosmic Liturgy, because the sacrifice of Jesus has a cosmic dimension of redeeming and restoring the whole of creation in Him and through Him. St. Paul, taking to heart the universality of the sacrifice of Jesus, his exaltation and Lordship in the Eucharistic celebration, concluded, "Every knee shall bend of those in heaven, and on earth, and under the earth" (Philippians 2:10).

3. Sitting

Sitting is a posture that points to attentive listening and meditation. "She had a sister called Mary, who was seated at the Lord's feet, listening to His word" (Luke: 10:39). Mary, the sister of Martha and Lazarus, sat at the Lord's feet, assuming the posture of a disciple because she loved Jesus with all her heart and soul. During Mass, the assembly sits for the readings before the Gospel and the homily. They may also sit during the period of meditation after communion.

4. Gestures

Gestural theory of language evolution states that gestures were the precursor to language. Robert Krauss of Columbia University concluded one of his papers with this story:

Many years ago, my maternal grandfather told me a story about two men in his hometown, Vitebsk, Belorussia, walking down a road on a bitterly cold winter day. One man chattered away animatedly, while other nodded from time to time, but said nothing. Finally, the man who was talking turned to his friend and said: "So, nu, Shmuel, why aren't you saying anything?" "Because," replied Shmuel, "I forgot my gloves."

At the time, I didn't see the point of the story. Half a century later it has become a primary focus of my research.

So, by gesturing you not only unfreeze your body, you unfreeze your mind. According to Olivia Mitchell, there are three benefits of gesturing.

First, gesturing helps you to be fluent and articulate.

Second, it conveys energy and enthusiasm to the audience.

Third, gesturing makes you look confident. Francois Rabelais wrote, "Gestures, in love, are incomparably more attractive, effective and valuable than words."

It takes a lot of planning and creativity to make Liturgy an experience of the heart and powerfully evocative. Judith Kubicki narrates an experience she had in her hometown of Buffalo, New York, that powerfully conveyed the effectiveness of the message, when gestures are fully harmonized with words:

At the door of St. Joseph's Church, greeters offered each person a copy of the reading of the Passion. In my past experience, the assembly is usually assigned the parts of the rabble-rousing crowd, the "bad guys." To my surprise and delight, however, the congregation was assigned the part of Jesus Christ. Just think about that for a moment. Usually the part of Christ is automatically assigned to the priest. But in this case, the church community took the part of Christ. Such a gesture says volumes about how this parish (or the liturgy planning team) understood the assembly as the body of Christ, truly an instance of the presence of Christ in that time and place. The message, both verbal and nonverbal, was loud and clear.

When Jorge Bergoglio stepped onto the balcony at the Vatican on Wednesday to reveal himself as the new leader of the world's 1.2 billion Catholics, he quickly made history breaking with a few traditions in his first public act before the 150,000 people packed into St. Peter's Square. Rather than bless the crowd first, he asked them to pray for him.

"Let us say this prayer, your prayer for me, in silence," he told the cheering crowd. Pope elect also broke with another tradition by refusing to use a platform to elevate himself above the cardinals standing with him as he was introduced as Pope Francis.

A Vatican spokesman interpreted this as a sign of the new Pope's willingness at the outset to break with tradition and chart his own path in other ways. Pope Francis impresses and inspires more people with his evocative gestures than his articulate words.

Sign of the Cross is the most familiar gesture Catholics all over the world practice multiple times a day. It is an ancient practice and prayer. Bert Ghezzi, author of *Sign of the Cross: Recovering the Power of the Ancient Prayer*, describes six meanings, with and without words to this treasured gesture of faith. The Sign of the Cross is a confession of faith, a renewal of baptism, a mark of discipleship, an acceptance of suffering, a defense against the devil, and a victory over self-indulgence.

He further stated, "When you make the sign of the cross, you are professing a mini version of the creed—belief in the Father, and in the Son and in the Holy Spirit." The congregation makes the Sign of the Cross at the beginning and at the end of the Mass. The gesture is also made during the Sprinkling rite as well as upon entering the Church.

After saying, "A Reading from the Holy Gospel according to . . . ," the priest or deacon who proclaims the Gospel makes the Sign of the Cross, together with the assembly, with the thumb on the forehead, lips and breast. The significance of the threefold signing is that we want to (1) hear the Holy Gospel with an open mind, (2) proclaim it with our lips, and (3) cherish and safeguard it in our hearts. We are entreating the Lord for the grace to receive, acknowledge, and then profess the faith that we received in the Holy Gospel through our Lord, Jesus Christ, the Word of God incarnate.

Genuflection is an act of honor or worship. In the Bible, kneeling or genuflecting is done as a token of submission and reverence to God. According to the *General Instruction of the Roman Missal*:

A genuflection, made by bending the right knee to the ground, signifies adoration, and therefore it is reserved for the Most Blessed Sacrament, as well as for the Holy Cross from the solemn adoration during the liturgical celebration on Good Friday until the beginning of the Easter Vigil (274).

We Catholics, upon entering the church, before taking our seat, genuflect toward the Blessed Sacrament reserved inside the tabernacle. During the Eucharistic Prayer, the priest genuflects three times in adoration of the Blessed Sacrament: First, after showing the Sacred Host and then second, after elevating the Chalice, and again third, before Communion with the invitation and prayer, "Lord, I am not worthy. . . ."

If a tabernacle with the Blessed Sacrament is present in the sanctuary, a genuflection is made before and after Mass and whenever anyone passes in front of the Blessed Sacrament. Even when not participating at Mass, one should always adore the Blessed Sacrament whenever entering a Church, either by genuflecting toward the tabernacle or visiting the Blessed Sacrament chapel. If one is unable to genuflect, a reverent bow is an appropriate substitute.

Bowing—There are many ways to communicate without words. A kiss, a smile, the movements of the eyes, a handshake, and head movements. These are just some of the nonverbal ways people communicate to one another without ever uttering a word.

In Asian countries, bowing the head is the traditional way of greeting someone. In the Indian tradition, people greet one another with a bow accompanied by the word, 'Namaste,' which literally means, "I bow to you." Another deeper translation of this gesture, "My divine soul recognizes the divine soul in you," is inspiring and very much in keeping with Hindu faith.

Bowing is a gesture of reverence. "Bowing is a practice that will impart to you the humility, discipline, and acceptance you need to really see the beauty of life," writes Ilchi Lee. "Through its symbolic representation of the greater meaning of life's cyclical process, bowing will give you the faith and hope that you need, to keep going forward."

In the Western cultures, bowing has evolved differently. Bowing to one's superiors was part of the feudal European culture, but today bowing has become less common than it was. Europe will bow to queens or kings in their country, even though they are in most situations just titular heads, with no real power vested in them. People in West will bow as a sign of humility and gratefulness when they are applauded after a performance. In the West, we do not see the form of deep bow today except in theatres or in Churches before God.

Article 275 of the *General Instruction on the Roman Missal* addresses two distinctive types of bowing:

A bow signifies reverence and honor shown to the persons themselves or to the signs that represent them. There are two kinds of bow: a bow of the head and a bow of the body.
a) A bow of the head is made when the three Divine Persons are named together and at the names of Jesus, of the Blessed Virgin Mary, and of the Saint in whose honor Mass is being celebrated.
b) A bow of the body, that is to say, a profound bow, is made to the altar; during the prayers, *"Munda cor meum"* ("Cleanse my heart") and *"In spiritu humilitatis"* ("With humble spirit"); in the Creed at the words, *"et incarnatus est"* ("and by the Holy Spirit . . . and became man"); in the Roman Canon at the *"Supplices te rogamus"* ("In humble prayer we ask you, almighty God"). The same kind

of bow is made by the Deacon when he asks for a blessing before the proclamation of the Gospel. In addition, the Priest bows slightly as he pronounces the words of the Lord at the Consecration.

Striking the breast during the Confiteor—During the *Confiteor* ("I confess to Almighty God"), everyone strikes the breast at the words, "through my fault." In this profound gesture, one takes the right hand, curls it into a loose fist and strikes the left breast. In the Book of Jeremiah 31:19, the author wrote: "After I strayed, I repented; after I came to understand, I beat my breast. I was ashamed and humiliated because I bore the disgrace of my youth." In Gospel of Luke, while describing the publican's sense of sin and humility, the Evangelist wrote, "But the tax collector, standing some distance away, was even unwilling to lift up his eyes to heaven, but was beating his breast, saying, 'God, be merciful to me, the sinner'" (18: 10-14). Striking the breast is a sign of sorrow for one's sinfulness. The United States Conference of Catholic Bishops has noted: "During the Confiteor, the action of striking our breasts at the words *through my own fault* can strengthen my awareness that *my* sin is *my* fault."

5. Routine and Ritual

I would like to draw a contrast between ritual and routine. Routines are habits we form in our day-to-day lives. For example, getting up in the morning, brushing your teeth, having a shower, eating breakfast, and going to work is a routine in many people's lives. Routine is a sequence of actions regularly followed. There is no deeper meaning in routine.

Ritual is a religious or solemn ceremony, performed according to a prescribed order. The main difference between ritual and routine lies in the attitude behind them. Routine is a series of automatic actions whereas rituals refer to a series of meaningful actions. In the words of Henry Van Dyke, "As long as habit and routine dictate the pattern of living, new dimensions of the soul will not emerge." If one approaches Mass as a matter of routine, devoid of devotion and faith, it can never be an outward sign of inward or invisible grace.

The Office of Catholic Education in the Archdiocese of Brisbane put it this way:

> Ritual is so important in moving us from the everyday routines of our lives into that other realm where we become aware of who we are in the midst of a grander scheme, and a reality beneath reality. Ritual gives meaning amid the mundane. Christian ritual in prayer connects personal reality to a communal experience of reality involving words, gestures, words and objects in response to the presence of Christ among the gathered.

Conclusion

Liturgical body language unites the assembly and communicates deference for the liturgy, the community and for God. Through our postures and gestures we are totally involved—body, mind and spirit—in the act of worship. Liturgical postures and gestures emphasize the sense of transcendence and beauty in the celebration of the Sacraments. Pope Benedict XVI wrote in *Sacramentum Caritatis*:

> The Synod of Bishops asked that the faithful be helped to make their interior dispositions correspond to their gestures and words. . . . This is particularly important in a highly technological age like our own, which risks losing the ability to appreciate signs and symbols" (64).

Gestures are always better than words. They address more fully of our relationships, warmth, and unity in Christ, than our agreed declarations or dialogues do. Howard Gorle in his book, *Ceremonies and Rituals for Connection and Change*, draws a powerful lesson from the performing arts to make a point:

> Think of the performing arts. There are numerous pianists and singers who, although technically correct, fail to **connect** with an audience. An artist 'reads' (assigns value and meaning) to the words and score,

and somehow (gnosis) connects with deep emotions, memories, joys, and pains deep within me. I cry, laugh, "mellow out," or "chill baby." Is the agent of change (sacrament) the script or is it the "power" of the interpreter of the script? Is it possible to be an agent of change or "Living Sacrament" by simply "being"?

Every time Jesus reached out and healed, banishing sickness, hunger, even death itself, he was practicing the body language of conspicuous compassion. He reached out his hand and calmed the sea, exorcised demons in Jews and Gentiles alike, touched a woman who was ritually unclean because of her bleeding, and took a child by the hand to say, *"Talitha cum"* ("Little girl, get up"). Jesus reaches out to unclean people in the body language of conspicuous compassion. Throughout the Gospels, we get a glimpse of the body language of Jesus as he ministered among the people. Rev. Dr. Steven E. Albertin said in one his sermons, "With his body, in his body, through his body, a body that will be nailed to the cross and a body that will be raised again three days later, Jesus rescues those whom the world has forgotten."

Learning the Eucharistic body language, which is taken from Jesus himself—a language of unconditional love, faithful service, and loving sacrifice—can help build a better world. We are His body in the world. Through our body language, our actions, gestures and deeds, we continue the mission of Jesus. Through our body language, we demonstrate that this body, the mystical body of Christ which is us, is like no other. Is our body language consistent with the Gospel we preach? Is the corporate body language of the Church, which is the body of Christ consistent with the language of compassion, unconditional love, and at the same time a language that expresses inclusion?

Have you ever been in the situation when you really didn't believe what someone was saying? Did you have a sense that something didn't ring true or a gut feeling that all was not right? Perhaps they were saying, "Yes," while their heads were shaking, "No"? The difference between the words people speak and our understanding of what they are saying comes from nonverbal communication, otherwise known as "body language." By developing your awareness of the signs and signals of body language, you can more easily understand other people, and more effectively communicate with them. This is an area that, as a diocese and as individual parishes, we need to pay attention to.

Body language impacts a great deal of how we communicate with our congregation, the visitors in our midst, and more especially those who are in difficult or irregular situations of life, people who carry the baggage of shame and sin. Nonverbal communication includes body movements and gestures, Additionally, the tone of voice, the rate of speech and the pitch of the voice all add to the words that are being used.

In conversations, homilies and speeches, Pope Francis relies on animation, vocal emphasis, gestures, and spontaneous interjections to get his message across. This makes him a fascinating voice to listen to. More often than not, the only body language that parishes worry about is the body count. The more the bodies at liturgical services, the more successful the parish is thought to be. What really matters is that, as Christ's body, the Church strives to reflect Him and his language of love.

I would like to conclude with the words of St. Teresa of Avila:

Christ has no body now but yours.
No hands, no feet on earth but yours.
Yours are the eyes through which he looks compassion on this world.
Yours are the feet with which he walks to do good.
Yours are the hands through which he blesses all the world.
Yours are the hands, yours are the feet, yours are the eyes, you are his body.
Christ has no body now on earth but yours.

Indeed, it is our calling to live out the truth that we in the Church are the Mystical Body of Christ.

About the Author

Paulson Mundanmani is a Roman Catholic priest, pastor, and teacher. His passion for imparting a deeper understanding of the liturgy of the Mass to Catholics in the pews led him to research, write, and share *Bread Blessed and Broken for the World*.

The seventh of nine children born to Anthony and Elizabeth Mundanmani, his career as a priest and teacher has included work in education and both governmental and nongovernmental agencies in his native India. He was a consultant to "Misereor International" (The German Catholic Bishop's Organization for Development Cooperation), with a focus on technical training projects. In that capacity, he applied his leadership skills to shaping the vision and mission of SKIP (Skills For Progress), a conglomerate of nearly 200 technical institutions imparting employment-oriented skills training to the young, especially the poor.

He was educated by the Salesian Fathers of Don Bosco, with whom he worked for many years in the Northeastern Region of India. He held the position of General Manager of Don Bosco Technical School, Shillong, before transitioning to the United States of America.

Over the past twenty years, he has served the people of the Diocese of Oakland, California, and currently pastors Christ the King Community in Pleasant Hill. He has also ministered as a parish priest at St. Mary Catholic Church (Walnut Creek), St. Isidore (Danville), Holy Spirit (Fremont), and St. Edward (Newark).

He served as a consultor to the Bishop of Oakland and sat on the Priests' Advisory Council. He is currently Chaplain to Catholics at Work, a diocesan ministry that encourages and supports business people and professionals in industry and other endeavors to close the gap between corporate life and commitment to their faith.

In addition to degrees in theology and philosophy, Fr. Paulson holds an MBA in Human Resources Management from Indira Gandhi's National Open University (IGNOU), Delhi, India, and doctoral degree in Catholic Educational Leadership from the University of San Francisco.